"It's well known that the Hebrew word for *spirit* is also the word for *wind* and for *breath*, but I don't think anyone has done as much with that fact as Jack Levison in this book. He shows how the word *rûaḥ* speaks of the spiritual and the material not as two separate things but as related facets of the way that God in his liveliness involves himself in the world. It is appropriate that this book on the spirit should be inspiring. A beautiful combination of the academic and the nurturing, it works by careful, thoughtful, life-giving study of whole passages where *rûaḥ* appears, and it invites measured and reflective assimilation."

—**John Goldingay**, Fuller Theological Seminary

"*A Boundless God* offers us a careful study of *rûaḥ* from the Jewish Scriptures that takes the reader on a journey into an expansive vision for what is meant by talk of the breath, wind, spirit, or Spirit of God. Jack Levison demonstrates the depth and breadth of the rich and full experience of God as Spirit and of God and spirit in bringing humanity to the fullness of life. Readers will be challenged to lay down old paradigms and dichotomies and to embrace an understanding of the spirit that is far more nuanced than before, all while being confronted with a vibrant, fresh, and life-filled vision of how God moves among his creation in and by the spirit."

—**Lucy Peppiatt**, Westminster Theological Centre, United Kingdom

"It's easy for Christians to imagine that in the Old Testament the holy spirit is mostly waiting in the wings until a grand entrance can be made in the New Testament. But in *A Boundless God* Jack Levison shows this to be entirely false. From the spirit that broods over the face of the deep in Genesis to a remnant of the spirit found in Malachi, the Old Testament is saturated with the holy breath, wind, and spirit of God. *A Boundless God* is a remarkable achievement, alerting the reader to the ubiquitous and transforming presence of the holy spirit throughout the Old Testament."

—**Brian Zahnd**, pastor of Word of Life Church, St. Joseph, Missouri; author of *Postcards from Babylon*

A Boundless
GOD

A Boundless
GOD

THE SPIRIT
according to the
OLD TESTAMENT

JACK LEVISON

B
Baker Academic
a division of Baker Publishing Group
Grand Rapids, Michigan

© 2020 by Jack Levison

Published by Baker Academic
a division of Baker Publishing Group
PO Box 6287, Grand Rapids, MI 49516-6287
www.bakeracademic.com

Printed in the United States of America

Library of Congress Cataloging-in-Publication Data
Names: Levison, John R., author.
Title: A boundless God : the Spirit according to the Old Testament / Jack Levison.
Description: Grand Rapids, MI : Baker Academic, a division of Baker Publishing
    Group, [2020] | Includes index.
Identifiers: LCCN 2019027442 | ISBN 9781540961181 (paperback)
Subjects: LCSH: Bible. Old Testament—Theology. | Ruaḥ (The Hebrew word) | Spirit—
    Biblical teaching. | Holy Spirit—Biblical teaching.
Classification: LCC BS1199.S69 L48 2020 | DDC 221.6—dc23
LC record available at https://lccn.loc.gov/2019027442

ISBN 978-1-5409-6266-9 (casebound)

20   21   22   23   24   25   26   7   6   5   4   3   2   1

To Eugene Peterson

(1932–2018)

a kindred spirit

Contents

Acknowledgments

On the night before she delivered the presidential address at the Wesleyan Theological Society, my wife, Priscilla, met with Bob Hosack of Baker Academic. Priscilla had invited me to join them for dinner; there, in Cleveland, Tennessee, Bob and I had our first opportunity to discuss this book over a particularly pleasant meal. Bob is indefatigable—and savvy. It is grim work to secure a contract in today's book market, yet Bob managed to sign me on to two. Deep thanks to Bob for managing this feat and for shepherding me so deftly through the early stages of publication with Baker Academic.

The rest of the Baker Academic team has also done terrific work: Jeremy Wells, Mason Slater, Shelly MacNaughton, and Kara Day in marketing; Jennifer Hale and John Simpson in editing; and Paula Gibson in cover design. There will be more as the publication date approaches, and I am sure they will approach their tasks with similar enthusiasm and expertise.

Many thanks to Paraclete Press and to Eerdmans for their permission to echo some of the ideas found in my earlier books *Filled with the Spirit* (Eerdmans, 2009), *Fresh Air: The Holy Spirit for an Inspired Life* (Paraclete, 2012), *Inspired: The Holy Spirit and the Mind of Faith* (Eerdmans, 2013), and *40 Days with the Holy Spirit: Fresh Air for Every Day* (Paraclete, 2015).

Thanks as well to Perkins School of Theology for a Scholarly Outreach Award, which made possible a summer free of teaching and full of research. I am grateful in particular to Craig Hill, dean of Perkins

School of Theology, Southern Methodist University, for the privilege of a yearlong research leave, during which time I tackled projects I never could have otherwise. This has not been a particularly relaxing sabbatical, but it has been a productive one.

Under the auspices of the W. J. A. Power Chair of Old Testament Interpretation and Biblical Hebrew, I was able to edit this book thoroughly, one last time, in a Tuscan villa perched high along the ancient city walls of Barga, Italy. The Community of Jesus, whose Paraclete Press published my *Fresh Air* and *40 Days with the Holy Spirit*, owns this villa, and some members of the Community of Jesus staff it. These half dozen good and generous souls exhibited unimaginable hospitality, which made the otherwise arduous task of editing a sheer pleasure.

My gratitude also to Loren Stuckenbruck, thanks to whom Priscilla and I worked at the Ludwig-Maximilians-Universität in Munich on a generous resumption of my Alexander von Humboldt fellowship. There, minutes from the English Garden and far too close to Wimmer Bäkerei for my own good, I readied this book for publication.

Bart Patton, a terrific colleague and a whiz on his laptop, created the graphs in this book. Perhaps anyone could have figured out how to make the bar graph, but it took someone with Bart's wherewithal to imagine the other.

Thanks, finally, to my family. Chloe and Jeremy surprised me by moving to Dallas—both of them—after I took up my position at SMU in 2015. They keep me honest, keep me laughing, and keep me humble by not taking me too seriously. Then there is Priscilla, whose sixtieth birthday we celebrated Saturday night with beach volleyball and Scottish country dancing in a labyrinth. Gazing into her eyes as we danced, I could have been thirty again, when Priscilla and I spent a blustery and breathtaking year in St. Andrews. The travels we have taken, that beautiful mild woman and I, the adventures we have known. I am grateful for that—for *her*—too.

Abbreviations

General

alt.	altered
ed.	edition; edited by
esp.	especially
ET	English Translation
MT	Masoretic Text (Hebrew and Aramaic)

Bible Versions

CEB	Common English Bible
NETS	New English Translation of the Septuagint
NIV	New International Version
NRSV	New Revised Standard Version

Old Testament

Gen.	Genesis	2 Sam.	2 Samuel
Exod.	Exodus	1 Kings	1 Kings
Lev.	Leviticus	2 Kings	2 Kings
Num.	Numbers	1 Chron.	1 Chronicles
Deut.	Deuteronomy	2 Chron.	2 Chronicles
Josh.	Joshua	Ezra	Ezra
Judg.	Judges	Neh.	Nehemiah
Ruth	Ruth	Esther	Esther
1 Sam.	1 Samuel	Job	Job

Ps(s).	Psalm(s)	Amos	Amos
Prov.	Proverbs	Obad.	Obadiah
Eccles.	Ecclesiastes	Jon.	Jonah
Song	Song of Songs	Mic.	Micah
Isa.	Isaiah	Nah.	Nahum
Jer.	Jeremiah	Hab.	Habakkuk
Lam.	Lamentations	Zeph.	Zephaniah
Ezek.	Ezekiel	Hag.	Haggai
Dan.	Daniel	Zech.	Zechariah
Hosea	Hosea	Mal.	Malachi
Joel	Joel		

New Testament

Matt.	Matthew	1 Tim.	1 Timothy
Mark	Mark	2 Tim.	2 Timothy
Luke	Luke	Titus	Titus
John	John	Philem.	Philemon
Acts	Acts	Heb.	Hebrews
Rom.	Romans	James	James
1 Cor.	1 Corinthians	1 Pet.	1 Peter
2 Cor.	2 Corinthians	2 Pet.	2 Peter
Gal.	Galatians	1 John	1 John
Eph.	Ephesians	2 John	2 John
Phil.	Philippians	3 John	3 John
Col.	Colossians	Jude	Jude
1 Thess.	1 Thessalonians	Rev.	Revelation
2 Thess.	2 Thessalonians		

Old Testament Pseudepigrapha

Jub.   *Jubilees*

Dead Sea Scrolls

1QS   *Community Rule*
1QSb   *Rule of the Blessing*

Introduction

Wordplay

The Jewish Scriptures, what Christians call the Old Testament, include some evocative words. Words like *shalom* and *Sabbath*. *Torah*. *Covenant* or *testament*. *Blessing* and *mercy*. These are more than mere words. They are ciphers, signifiers, pointers to a consequential world apart that becomes a part of Israel's world. Words such as these are like old-fashioned keyholes through which you could peek and see a hidden room. In our parlance, they function like hyperlinks, opening to a reservoir of meaning. These key nouns punctuate the pages of the Jewish Scriptures:

- *bərākâ*: blessing, occurs 71 times
- *šabbāt̲*: Sabbath, occurs 111 times
- *kāb̲ôd̲*: glory, occurs 200 times
- *tôrâ*: Torah, teaching, or law, occurs 223 times
- *šālôm*: *shalom*, peace, well-being, or simply *hello!*, occurs 237 times
- *ḥesed̲*: mercy or covenant faithfulness, occurs 249 times
- *bərît̲*: covenant or agreement, occurs 287 times
- *rûaḥ*: breath, wind, or spirit, occurs 378 times in Hebrew and 11 times in Aramaic[1]

1. These numbers are based upon Accordance software, although I also have consulted Ludwig Koehler and Walter Baumgartner, *The Hebrew and Aramaic Lexicon*

Of these nouns, the one that occurs most frequently is *rûaḥ*: five times more often than the word for *blessing*, three times more than *Sabbath*, nearly twice as many as *Torah*.

You will not see this huge number in English Bibles, where the Hebrew word *rûaḥ* is translated by different words. In English, the 389 occurrences of *rûaḥ* tend to be subdivided into *breath*, *wind*, *spirit*, and *Spirit*; sometimes *rûaḥ* is not translated by any of these words, such as when the Hebrew phrase *spirit of wisdom* is translated simply as *skill*.[2] Not so in Hebrew, a language in which the word *rûaḥ* has much broader shoulders than any one of these English words. *Rûaḥ*, simply put, carries more weight than English translations can communicate.[3]

We can illustrate the dominance of *rûaḥ* with a simple bar graph, where the occurrences of the word *rûaḥ* eclipse other significant words in the Jewish Scriptures (fig. 1). A more dramatic illustration

---

of the Old Testament (Leiden: Brill, 1994). Though relatively secure, there may be slight variations because of differences among the manuscripts. I've used English translations from the NRSV throughout the manuscript, though I modify this translation when necessary.

2. This occurs in the NRSV translation of Exod. 28:3. The NIV translates the phrase with *wisdom* and the CEB with *special abilities*.

3. You will notice that the word *spirit* is typically not capitalized in this book. The primary reason is that the Jewish Scriptures are full of surprises, making an easy decision about capitalization impossible. For example, you will see right off the bat in chap. 1 how a "wind from the LORD" comes from the sea. Should *wind* be capitalized because it is from the Lord? Or what about the breath? If every breath is from God, should *breath* be capitalized? Along the same vein, *rûaḥ*, because it is such a powerful word, defies neat dichotomies between divine and human, spiritual and physical. Therefore, rather than choosing to capitalize some references, presumably because they refer to God's Spirit, and leaving others uncapitalized, presumably because they refer to the human spirit or breath or the wind, I have chosen the path of consistency. This allows you as the reader—rather than me as the translator—to make your own decision about the meaning of *rûaḥ*.

This much will become clear: in the Old Testament, *rûaḥ* shatters—perhaps a better word is *transcends*—the feeble dichotomies with which it is so easy otherwise to operate. The nearly four hundred references to *rûaḥ* in the Old Testament cannot easily be sliced and diced into breath, wind, spirit, and Spirit. You need not take my word for it; much of the territory ahead of us will make this case, starting with chap. 1. If you would like to read more about this decision, I have discussed it in much more detail in *Filled with the Spirit* (Grand Rapids: Eerdmans, 2009), 36–41. Particularly if you are prone to disagree with my decision not to capitalize *spirit*, I highly commend that discussion to you.

The Dominance of *Rûaḥ*

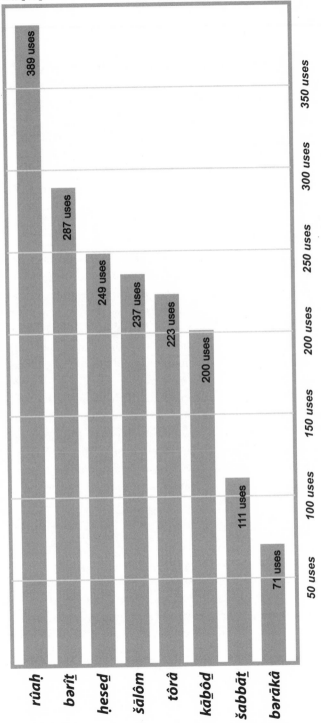

- rûaḥ — 389 uses
- bərît — 287 uses
- ḥeseḏ — 249 uses
- šālôm — 237 uses
- tôrâ — 223 uses
- kāḇôḏ — 200 uses
- šabbāt — 111 uses
- barākâ — 71 uses

50 uses 100 uses 150 uses 200 uses 250 uses 300 uses 350 uses

Bart Patton

includes some of the world's iconic landmarks (fig. 2). If each occur-rence of *rûaḥ* were calculated to equal slightly more than three feet in height, then the 389 occurrences of the word *rûaḥ* would rise to the height of the Empire State Building. The Hebrew word for *cov-enant* would be as tall as the Eiffel Tower, while the Hebrew word for *mercy* would reach to the tip of the Transamerica Pyramid in San Francisco. The seemingly ubiquitous word *shalom* reaches only to the top of the Golden Gate Bridge—high enough but not nearly as high as the Empire State Building. *Torah* is the height of the St. Louis Gateway Arch, while *glory* reaches to the top of the Space Needle in Seattle, *Sabbath* to the flame of the Statue of Liberty, and *blessing* to the highest peak of the Taj Mahal.

The 378 occurrences of the Hebrew word *rûaḥ*, plus another eleven Aramaic instances in the book of Daniel, render *rûaḥ* a dominant—*imposing* might be an even better description—noun, overshadowing other momentous nouns in the Hebrew Bible. Trying to understand the Old Testament without the dominance of *rûaḥ* is like trying to imagine New York City without the Empire State Building. Yet *rûaḥ* should be more than dominant; it should be *iconic*. Still, in an ironic and unfortunate state of affairs, there is actually a disconcerting disparity between the prominence of the word *rûaḥ* in the Old Tes-tament and the near absence of the Old Testament in studies of the spirit. The effect is a truncated study of the spirit, whose contours are too easily shaped by later literature, such as the New Testament, without serious and sustained consideration of the nearly four hun-dred references to *rûaḥ* that lie at the base of the Jewish Scriptures.

Hostile Territory

Trying to understand the spirit as if the word *rûaḥ* did not occur 389 times in the Jewish Bible makes no sense. Starting anywhere other than the Jewish Scriptures, in fact, makes no sense in light of the founda-tional role these Scriptures play in the formation of Judaism and Chris-tianity. Yet many Christian studies of the spirit[4] begin with only a quick

---

4. Christian theologians call study of the holy spirit *pneumatology*, based upon the Greek word for *spirit* or *breath*: *pneuma*.

The Dominance of *Rûaḥ*

rûaḥ
Empire State Building
1,250 ft.
(roof height)
389 uses
x 3.21 ft. =
1,250

barît
Eiffel Tower
984 ft.
(roof height)
287 uses
x 3.21 ft. =
921
(margin of 63 ft.)

ḥeseḏ
Transamerica Pyramid
853 ft.
249 uses
x 3.21 ft. =
799
(margin of 54 ft.)

šālôm
Golden Gate Bridge
746 ft.
237 uses
x 3.21 ft. =
761
(margin of 15 ft.)

tôrâ
Gateway Arch
630 ft.
223 uses
x 3.21 ft. =
716
(margin of 86 ft.)

kāḇôḏ
Space Needle
605 ft.
200 uses
x 3.21 ft. =
642
(margin of 37 ft.)

šabbāṯ
Statue of Liberty
305 ft.
111 uses
x 3.21 ft. =
356
(margin of 51 ft.)

bərākâ
Taj Mahal
240 ft.
71 uses
x 3.21 ft. =
228
(margin of 12 ft.)

1,250 ft.

1,000 ft.

750 ft.

500 ft.

250 ft.

glance at the Jewish Scriptures,[5] and the spirit in the Jewish Scriptures is the topic of only a handful of books in English.[6] The neglect of *rûaḥ* in studies of the Jewish Scriptures is nothing short of tragic.

It is also dangerous. Let me illustrate this with a cautionary tale. During the 1930s, under the sway of national socialism, a cadre of German scholars and theologians—and many of the German people with them—detached Christianity from its Jewish heritage. The Godesberg Declaration, published in 1939, portrayed Christianity as "the unbridgeable religious opposition to Judaism." On all sorts of levels, Jesus was stripped of his Jewishness. For example, some professors appealed to the diverse population in Galilee in Jesus's day to argue that his parents could not have been Jews by race. Popular authors, too, joined the fray. One allegory, which sold more than a quarter of a million copies by 1944, with translations into forty languages, reconceived Jesus as a savior born in Schleswig-Holstein. Even artists bent to the will of Nazi ideology. At the 1937 Nazi exhibit of "Degenerate Art," Christ's anguish on the cross was considered unacceptable. He was to be portrayed as aggressive and masculine; even on the cross, he was to be a strong Aryan. For example, in a wall mural in the Lutherkirche in Offenbach-Bieber, Jesus has Aryan features while the thief next to him is hunched over with exaggerated features as a European Jew.[7]

What happened when scholars, authors, artists, and pastors jettisoned Jesus's Jewishness? We know the answer to this question. We understand the cultural captivity of Christ and where it led.

5. For example, Yves Congar devotes a dozen pages to the Old Testament in his massive *I Believe in the Holy Spirit* (New York: Crossroad, 1999), 3–14; Sergius Bulgakov devotes four to the topic in his dense and long *The Comforter* (Grand Rapids: Eerdmans, 2004), 156–59.

6. Lloyd Neve, *The Spirit of God in the Old Testament* (Cleveland: CPT, 2011); Wilf Hildebrandt, *An Old Testament Theology of the Spirit of God* (Peabody, MA: Hendrickson, 1995); Christopher Wright, *Knowing the Holy Spirit through the Old Testament* (Downers Grove, IL: IVP Academic, 2006). Some books on the spirit analyze both testaments. For example, George Montague, *Holy Spirit: Growth of a Biblical Tradition* (Peabody, MA: Hendrickson, 1976); Michael Welker, *God the Spirit* (Minneapolis: Fortress, 1994); Levison, *Filled with the Spirit*. David Firth and Paul Wegner have edited *Presence, Power, and Promise: The Role of the Spirit of God in the Old Testament* (Downers Grove, IL: InterVarsity, 2011).

7. Susannah Heschel includes this mural in *The Aryan Jesus: Christian Theologians and the Bible in Nazi Germany* (Princeton: Princeton University Press, 2008), 51, with a close-up on p. 54.

Along the same lines, to understand the holy spirit as an exclusively *Christian* entity, known principally from the New Testament and independent of the literature of Israel, is to enter dangerous territory. It opens the door to a spirit—and spirituality—that stands to serve a contemporary cultural goal, maybe even a sinister one. Without the perspective of an entire landscape, which the Jewish Scriptures provide, it becomes too easy, too *tempting*, to be altogether too selective in the dimensions of the spirit one chooses to emphasize or experience.

Developing an understanding of the spirit without the Jewish Scriptures is like living in a beautiful mountain range but only in a small, narrow, dark valley. That valley, rather than expanding the horizon, eclipses it; paradise, or what could be paradise, becomes an ideological and experiential prison, even if the occupants of that valley are unaware of their limitations.

We can put this more positively. To understand the spirit through the Jewish Scriptures is to garner altogether new insight that is otherwise inaccessible to us. The results will be enlivening; we rise through valleys and hillsides and hairpin turns at sunset. The results may even be alarming for their unfamiliarity and freshness. But one thing is sure. Our grasp of the spirit, by the time we arrive at the last page of this book, whether invigorating or disquieting—or both—will certainly be *biblical*, and perhaps even *boundless*.

Shared Legacy

This study can function as a foreground to the New Testament, though it is not intended as such. The spirit in the Jewish Scriptures is not merely a precursor to the spirit in the New Testament. It is not merely a shadow, or foreshadowing, of realities to come. A study of the spirit in the Jewish Scriptures offers insights and challenges in its own right.

New Testament authors did in fact cull from the Jewish Scriptures in order to clarify their own understanding of the spirit, and it is essential for Christians to consider the influence the Jewish Scriptures had on the New Testament. For example, Jesus's platform in the

Gospel of Luke begins with Isaiah 61:1–2, which he reads when he arrives at the synagogue in Nazareth: "The Spirit of the Lord is upon me, because he has anointed me to bring good news to the poor. He has sent me to proclaim release to the captives and recovery of sight to the blind, to let the oppressed go free, to proclaim the year of the Lord's favor" (Luke 4:18–19).[8] It is not possible to understand Jesus, as Luke portrays him, without setting Jesus's vision within the context of this pivotal text from the Jewish Scriptures.

When Peter, in the book of Acts, attempts to explain the events of Pentecost, he turns to the prophet Joel's vision that the spirit would be outpoured: "In the last days it will be, God declares, that I will pour out my Spirit upon all flesh, and your sons and your daughters shall prophesy, and your young men shall see visions, and your old men shall dream dreams. Even upon my slaves, both men and women, in those days I will pour out my Spirit; and they shall prophesy" (Acts 2:17–18).[9] Just as it is not possible to understand Jesus without key texts in the Jewish Scriptures, it is not possible to understand the early church as Luke portrays it without setting its inaugural experience within the context of this pivotal text from the Jewish Scriptures.

The Jewish Scriptures, therefore, prove essential for understanding the New Testament. They compose an indispensable foreground to the New Testament. *But that is not all they are.*

The Jewish Scriptures are also the foreground of Judaism itself. While the early church busied itself with understanding its experience of the spirit in light of the Jewish Scriptures, Jewish writers were occupied along a parallel vein. Alongside Christians, Jews laid claim to these same ancient Scriptures—and the spirit embraced within them. Hundreds of references to *rûaḥ* punctuate the pages of early Jewish literature.[10] For example, in Jewish scrolls found in

---

8. The quotation is not exact; Jesus omits a reference to the brokenhearted. The omission of the only words in Isa. 61:1–4 that could be construed as individualistic and emotional underscores the economic and societal dimension of Jesus's platform.

9. Joel 2:28–29 (MT 3:1–2). The quotation is not exact. Peter, in this sermon, actually adds a second reference to prophesying, presumably for emphasis.

10. Peter Schäfer offers the best study of the spirit in rabbinic Judaism, though it is in German: *Die Vorstellung vom heiligen Geist in der rabbinischen Literatur* (Munich: Kösel, 1972). A useful collection can be found in Gary Cage, *The Holy Spirit: A Sourcebook with Commentary* (Reno, NV: Charlotte House, 1995). The

caves alongside the Dead Sea, scrolls composed before the rise of the early church, a description of the inspired ruler of Isaiah 11 is applied to the leader of the congregation that probably met at Qumran over half a millennium after Isaiah 11 was written: "May He[11] give [you 'the spirit of coun]sel and may eternal might [rest upon you], the spirit of knowledge and the fear of God.' May 'righteousness be the belt [around your waist, and faithful]ness the belt around your loins.'"[12] In a different set of Jewish hymns—these are *not* from the Dead Sea—we discover again the language of Isaiah 11, not to portray a leader already alive, as at Qumran, but to describe a hoped-for ruler who would "not weaken in his days, (relying) upon his God, for God made him powerful in the holy spirit and wise in the counsel of understanding, with strength and righteousness."[13]

It is inaccurate, therefore, to view the Old Testament primarily as a precursor to the New. It exists in its own right, a testimony to the vitality of Israel's varied and long-held convictions about *rûaḥ*. Equally important, the Hebrew Scriptures are the inspiration for countless Jewish claims to *rûaḥ*. Belief in the spirit, even the holy spirit,[14] therefore, is a shared legacy of both Jews and Christians.

Key Dates

The empires that loom large in Israelite history are Assyria (especially during the 700s BCE), Babylon (especially at the start of the 500s BCE), Persia (from the end of the 500s into the 300s BCE), and Greece

---

best collection of Dead Sea Scrolls texts, with commentary, are in Eibert Tigchelaar, "Historical Origins of the Early Christian Concept of the Holy Spirit," in *The Holy Spirit, Inspiration, and the Cultures of Antiquity: Multidisciplinary Perspectives*, ed. Jörg Frey and John R. Levison, with Andrew Bowden (Berlin: de Gruyter, 2014).

11. God.

12. *Rule of the Blessing* (1QSb) 5.25–26. Allusions are to Isa. 11:2, 5. Translations of the Dead Sea Scrolls are from Martin Abegg, Michael Wise, and Edward Cook, *The Dead Sea Scrolls: A New English Translation*, rev. ed. (New York: HarperCollins, 2005). Brackets signify places where a text is damaged or missing and in need of reconstruction.

13. *Psalms of Solomon* 17:37. Translation from James H. Charlesworth, ed., *Old Testament Pseudepigrapha* (Garden City: Doubleday, 1985), 2:668.

14. This phrase occurs in Ps. 51:11 (MT 51:13) and Isa. 63:10–11.

and Syria (particularly during the 100s BCE). When you hear about seventh-century prophets, think Assyria. About exile, think Babylon. About restoration, Persia. About the Maccabean rebellion, Greece and Syria. Five events, which go hand in hand with these empires, are also essential for perspective.

- In 722/21 BCE Assyria destroyed the Northern Kingdom of Israel and threatened the Southern Kingdom.[15]
- In 597 BCE Babylon deported many Israelite leaders, including the prophet Ezekiel; ten years later, in 587/86 BCE, Babylon destroyed Jerusalem entirely.
- Nearly fifty years later, in 539 BCE, the new Persian ruler Cyrus authorized the exiles to go home and rebuild. Some Israelites in exile did just that; they returned to Palestine determined to rebuild Jerusalem.
- The perennial inability to get the job done leads to our next date, 445 BCE, and the mission of Nehemiah to rebuild Jerusalem.
- Finally, in 175 BCE a horrible ruler terrorized the Jews, prompting what turned out to be a surprisingly successful Maccabean rebellion in 167 BCE.

Beginning a book on the holy spirit with dates from Israelite history may seem odd. But doing this reflects the genius of the Jewish Bible, where tradition, confession, and theology—pneumatology even—combust in the context of human history.[16]

---

15. According to 1 Kings 12, the kingdom had split two hundred years earlier, after the death of Solomon.

16. Perhaps now is the right time to say that this study is based on the literature of Israel rather than on a reconstructed history of Israel. This is not, in other words, a quest for historical Israel's experience of the spirit. Certainly there is overlap between history and literature; it is important to grasp the nature of Babylonian exile, for example, to understand the oracles of Isa. 40–55 and to ascertain the challenges of reconstruction during the Persian era to appreciate Haggai's promise about the spirit. Yet, for the most part, my analysis is of the literature of Israel. When I discuss Joseph or Moses, I mean the figures portrayed in literature and not their putative historical selves, about whose existence there is simply too much scholarly disagreement. There are many excellent studies of Israel's history for those keen to explore it, of which I will list just a few: Martin Noth, *The History of Israel*, 2nd ed. (New York: Harper & Row, 1960); John Bright, *A History of Israel*, 4th ed. (Louisville: Westminster John

Imperfect Rows

Not long ago, songwriter Nichole Nordeman reflected eloquently on the challenge inherent in a study of the spirit. The spirit, she mused, is "wild and growing in imperfect rows."[17] A look at the passages about the spirit in the Old Testament, jagged as they are, suggests that she has captured the character of these imperfect rows.

It is even difficult to know, right from the start, what to call this Jewish Bible. *Old Testament*, a Christian term, can repel Jewish readers; it is also not entirely accurate, since different Christian churches include different books in their Old Testaments.[18] *Jewish Scriptures*, on the other hand, may come across as alien to potential Christian readers. *Hebrew Bible* is a good descriptive term—it excludes the Apocrypha, for example, and accurately describes the language of all but a few chapters—yet few contemporary readers, with the exception of scholars, would find it familiar or comfortable.[19]

Nor is there a flawless way to organize a book on the spirit in Israelite literature. Lloyd Neve chose chronology, though any reader who has dipped a toe in scholarship knows there is barely an ounce of consensus on the dating of Israelite literature. Tracing progression—or retrenchment, for that matter—in hundreds of passages that are so hard to date is notoriously difficult. Wilf Hildebrandt selected prominent themes based upon the spirit of God in creation, in God's people, in Israel's leadership, and in prophecy; this works well overall, although the subtopics for each theme are slightly haphazard. This,

---

Knox, 2000); John Hayes and J. Maxwell Miller, *A History of Ancient Israel and Judah*, 2nd ed. (Louisville: Westminster John Knox, 2006); Megan Moore and Brad Kelle, *Biblical History and Israel's Past: The Changing Study of the Bible and History* (Grand Rapids: Eerdmans, 2011); and Iain Provan, V. Philips Long, and Tremper Longman, *A Biblical History of Israel* (Louisville: Westminster John Knox, 2015).

17. She wrote this in an endorsement for my *Fresh Air: The Holy Spirit for an Inspired Life* (Brewster, MA: Paraclete, 2012).

18. The Orthodox and Roman Catholic churches, for example, include apocryphal books (e.g., Tobit, Sirach, Wisdom of Solomon) that mainline and evangelical Protestant churches typically do not include. This book, by the way, does not include a study of apocryphal texts. Montague's *Holy Spirit* does, and I analyze swaths of this literature in my books *The Spirit in First-Century Judaism* (Leiden: Brill, 1997) and *Filled with the Spirit*.

19. I have no strong preference and will refer to Israelite literature variously as the Hebrew Bible, Jewish Scriptures, and Old Testament.

of course, is the nature of the beast: probing a dominant component in a diverse collection of literary texts from nearly a millennium of a community's existence. Christopher Wright's study is topical too: the creating, empowering, prophetic, anointing, and coming spirit. These are broad categories—perhaps too broad. Empowering, for example, suits all of the other categories, since power is inherent in creation, prophecy, divine anointing, and the spirit promised. They are also so broad as to include texts that should not be grouped together, such as the artisans who constructed the tabernacle in the desert alongside the judges who led Israel before Israel had kings; both types of Israelites were empowered—but in extremely different ways. Artisans were *filled* with the spirit of wisdom; the spirit *rushed* or came upon or clothed the judges. The ends differed too; skilled artisans built a tabernacle, while judges liberated Israel with armies.[20]

I have organized this study around verbs associated with the spirit. This principle has flaws too, not least of which is how difficult it is to cover all 389 occurrences of *rûaḥ* in the Jewish Scriptures, though I intend those I cover to be representative of many, if not most, of what I do not cover.

Despite the challenges posed by a study of the spirit in the Jewish Scriptures, our knowledge of the spirit can flourish by rekindling the understanding that Israel, in various guises and places and eras, embraced. If we retrace our steps, which in a way is what these chapters do, and recapture Israel's tenacious sense of the *rûaḥ*'s presence, we can expect our grasp of the spirit to be informed, even supple,

20. In his section on the Old Testament, George Montague adopts an eclectic approach that evinces no dominant principle of organization. Chaps. 1 and 7 are chronological: the earliest traditions and voices of the restoration (pre-539 BCE). Chap. 2 looks at the book of Deuteronomy and various passages in Judges, 1–2 Samuel, and 1–2 Kings, which seem to be edited from the perspective of Deuteronomy. Chaps. 3 and 4 analyze prophetic literature, divided chronologically between preexilic prophets (pre-597 BCE), prophets of exile (597–539 BCE), and prophets of restoration (post-539 BCE). Chap. 5 explores what scholars have come to call the priestly tradition: a literary source from the period of restoration that includes several passages featuring the spirit (Exod. 31:3; Num. 16:22; 27:18; Gen. 1:2). Chaps. 8 and 9 are identified principally by literary genre. Chap. 8 examines apocalyptic literature; chap. 9 explores the wisdom tradition (e.g., Proverbs, Ecclesiastes, Job, Sirach [Ecclesiasticus], and Wisdom of Solomon). Chaps. 10 and 11 deal with postbiblical Judaism: rabbinic literature and the Dead Sea Scrolls.

like the spirit blowing, breathing, coming, resting, passing, pouring, filling, cleansing, leading, and guiding. This may not always be neat and tidy, despite my best effort, but, as Nichole Nordeman has said, we have occasion to study the spirit in order to "unearth its complex root system, and then marvel at the beauty that blooms above. Wild and growing in imperfect rows."[21]

---

21. Endorsement, Levison, *Fresh Air*.

1

Spirit Blowing and Breathing

> **Before reading this chapter, explore these texts:**
>
> » Genesis 1:1–2
> » Numbers 11:10–35
> » Job 12:7–10
> » Job 32:8–9
> » Psalm 104:27–30
> » Psalm 146:1–4
> » Ezekiel 37:1–14

Just seventy-two hours removed from Mount Sinai, on their dramatic and prolonged trek from Egypt to the promised land, the Israelites complained. They complained a good bit on this journey, but just seventy-two hours removed from the site of intense revelation seems a bit much. Their complaints appear to be the epitome of ingratitude, but their anxiety was not unfounded. The threat of desert sandstorms, only one of the perils they faced, can turn seventy-two minutes, let alone seventy-two hours, into a maelstrom of disorientation—and death. In 2012, twenty-three vehicles were involved in a series of crashes that killed one person and injured seventeen people near Lubbock, Texas, when a dust storm blanketed the region. "It was a white-out," claimed Corporal John Gonzalez. "You couldn't see past the hood of your vehicle."[1] During the blizzard of 1888, famously called the children's blizzard, boys and girls dismissed early from school perished while making their way home in the Dakotas and Minnesota. Some Scandinavian immigrants, hardly strangers to snowstorms, died walking from their back doors to their barns, so strong were the winds and severe the snow.[2]

Wind—*rûaḥ*—can be a relentless enemy and a fickle friend. Some scholars may tell us that the imperceptible physical movements of the palpable wind, of *rûaḥ*, metamorphosed over centuries of Israelite reflection into the movements of the invisible spirit, but this simple equation belies the unpredictability and menace of wind, which can turn a pleasant sojourn into a fatal expedition. Spirit, from this vantage point, is not a benign companion but a fierce escort, able to turn on a dime from breeze to blast. If wind is a force of nature, then spirit is a force of faith. Both, in the end, are *rûaḥ*.

Seventy-two hours removed from Mount Sinai, then, the Israelites had reason for concern, so they complained about the food. I am reminded by their complaint of a moment, toward the tail end of my days at Cambridge, when famed historian Owen Chadwick, master of Selwyn College, invited me to his rooms to tender a decision about a five-hundred pound travel grant I had applied for to study German in Münster. As we chatted, he said, "Students will always complain about something, so we make sure the food is not very good so that they will complain about something insignificant." The Israelites, like so many college students, complained about the food and yearned for the cuisine of home, even the fleshpots of Egypt. (By the way, I did not receive that grant. "We feel you can do this just as well," quipped Professor Chadwick memorably, "with a good grammar and a transistor radio.")

God reacted to Israel's grievance in a sequence of three acts. God countered first with a fire that spread—fire expands only through the agency of wind—around the outskirts of the camp (Num. 11:1–9).

1. "Snowstorm Causes Problems for Travelers in West," *Tampa Bay Times*, Dec. 20, 2012.

2. David Laskin offers a chilling narrative of this blizzard in *The Children's Blizzard* (New York: Harper, 2004).

This did nothing to assuage their hunger, so God took another tack, this one to allay the pressure on Moses by distributing the *rûaḥ* that was on Moses to seventy elders, who prophesied, along with two other elders, Eldad and Medad, who had not joined the seventy but prophesied anyway (making a total of seventy-two, like the hours since their respite at Sinai). A remarkable story to be sure, this relentless spread of *rûaḥ*. Yet this divine response failed again to ease their hunger (Num. 11:10–30), so finally, in a third scene, a *rûaḥ* "from the LORD" brought an unimaginably robust harvest of quail "from the sea and let them fall beside the camp, about a day's journey on this side and a day's journey on the other side, all around the camp, about two cubits deep on the ground" (Num. 11:31). The *rûaḥ* did the trick this time: hunger satisfied.

Three divine acts. A fire that spread implicitly through the agency of *rûaḥ*. A *rûaḥ* from Moses that caused a controlled epidemic of prophesying. And a *rûaḥ* that brought a waist-high delivery of meat. Elemental to all of these divine initiatives is *rûaḥ*, yet only one would normally attract the attention of a study of the Spirit in the Old Testament. Only one allegedly is spiritual. Only one inspires prophecy. Yet all of them are integral, each of them important, each an instructive and essential component for comprehending *rûaḥ*.

Together these stories communicate the incapacity of human beings to control *rûaḥ*: fire rips throughout the fringes of the camp, prophesying spreads from the outskirts to the camp, quail spread from the sea to encircle the camp. Over none of these experiences do human beings exercise control; they could not, even if they tried, forestall the fire or the prophesying or the nourishment.

There is also a fierceness to *rûaḥ* in this sequence of stories. Not so much in the first scene, where even a breeze could have made the fire spread. But in the second scene, *rûaḥ* had to leap past the wide ribbon of land that separated the two elders from the tent of meeting, where the seventy other elders prophesied in the presence of Moses. The third scene is also fierce: so many quail driven from the sea and deposited in such a swath of land! This is not a temperate breeze.

Something else arises from these stories: the presence of *rûaḥ* is lavish. The fire would have continued spreading had Moses not intervened to stop its spread. The *rûaḥ* was so plentiful that two elders far removed from the group of seventy began to prophesy; there was so much *rûaḥ*, in other words, that more than the intended seventy experienced the impact. And the quail, which *rûaḥ* transported from the sea, filled a day's journey from the camp, three feet deep. The image of Israelites wading waist-high through quail is almost comic. There is, again, more than enough *rûaḥ*—less like a breeze than a tornado. In each of these episodes, there is a surfeit of *rûaḥ*.

To these insights we may add an observation: any effort to subdivide *rûaḥ* into breath, wind, spirit, or Spirit is doomed to abject failure. In this story, or sequence of stories, *rûaḥ* defies categories and overruns tidy edges. The implicit presence of *rûaḥ* in the spread of fire, the advent of *rûaḥ* in communal prophesying, the arrival of dinner in a commanding display of *rûaḥ*—not one of these is any more or less *rûaḥ* than the other.

These stories throw into disarray efforts to slice and dice *rûaḥ* into breath, wind, spirit, and Spirit. There are elsewhere clear instances where *rûaḥ* is a wind—we might say merely a wind—or where *rûaḥ* is what keeps people alive—we might say merely breath—but the genius of the Jewish Scriptures is their ability, on the whole, to fuse these realities. When one scholar talks about *trifurcation* (that is his word), he means to distinguish the spirit *of* God from the wind and the spirit in creatures.[3] This will not do. Bifurcation or trifurcation is a violation of *rûaḥ*.

The mysterious world of the *rûaḥ* defies easy classification. The *rûaḥ* on Moses, we might think, is definitely God's spirit, given how closely *rûaḥ* is associated with prophesying. But to say this with certainty would also be ill-advised, because *rûaḥ* is not in this scene depicted unequivocally as God's spirit. God does not refer to *rûaḥ* as "*my* spirit, which is upon you," but more tersely—and ambiguously—as "*the* spirit that is on you" (Num. 11:17). This scene, then, which seems on the surface to feature unmistakably God's spirit with a capital S, proves more elusive; it is difficult to say with confidence that God distributes *God's* spirit to the elders. It may be that God distributes *Moses's* spirit, *Moses's* charisma, *Moses's* capacity to

---

3. Lloyd Neve, *The Spirit of God in the Old Testament* (Cleveland: CPT, 2011), 3–4. Neve's appeal to trifurcation is actually an effort to reduce the categories from four (wind, breath, spirit, Spirit) to three (wind, spirit in creatures, spirit of God).

prophesy to the elders so that they can help him manage his recalcitrant people.

The next scene, by contrast, seems to have nothing to do with God's spirit, since *rûaḥ* is clearly a wind, a force of nature, a material element sweeping in from the sea. Yet this *rûaḥ* is the only one in this sequence of events identified without a doubt as a *rûaḥ* "from the LORD." A wind from the sea is no *less* divine than a power that compels prophesying. By the same token, the power to prophesy is no *more* divine than a gale that supplies quail. To put this essential point another way, it is not the *rûaḥ* prompting prophesying but the *rûaḥ* dumping a boatload of quail around the camp that has exclusive rights to being named—to use traditional capitalization—the *Spirit* from the LORD.

Neat and tidy categorization, as natural as it may seem, does not do justice to the mysterious world of *rûaḥ* in the Jewish Scriptures. A penchant for clear categories, for bifurcation or trifurcation, may mislead us as we attempt to grasp this ancient reality. We might just overlook some essential texts, like the quail-infested *rûaḥ*-wind from the sea, or neglect the ambiguity of other texts, like the case of the prophesying elders.

With this perspective, we are ready to proceed in this study of the spirit in the Old Testament. What will drive our approach is not a proclivity for taxonomy but the tenor and tones of the stories, oracles, and poems through which a reader encounters *rûaḥ*, with its inexorable defiance of categories and classification.

Wind

Having said that, more than a third of the nearly four hundred references to *rûaḥ* in the Jewish Bible are to *rûaḥ* understood as a wind or breeze. The wicked are like chaff that the wind drives away (Ps. 1:4). A great wind causes Job's house to collapse (Job 1:19). The north wind brings rain (Prov. 25:23). Much of life is vanity and chasing after wind (Eccles. 1:14, 17). The east wind blows fiercely and frequently (Ezek. 17:10). Sin, like the wind, carries people away (Isa. 64:5). While wind can be a light breeze, a cool respite in a garden (Gen. 3:8), it is typically strong enough to carry chaff or, more impressively, to scatter ships (Ps. 48:7; MT 48:8).

Still, whatever the magnitude of this wind, we would be remiss to distance it from God. When clouds, wind, and rain fill the sky in Elijah's line of sight following a devastating drought, they are *God's* doing (1 Kings 18:45). Perhaps for this reason the winds are God's heavenly chariot. In a poetic stanza, in which the earth reeled and rocked, in which smoke ascended from God's nostrils and fierce fire from God's mouth, God "rode on a cherub, and flew" and "was seen upon the wings of the wind" (2 Sam. 22:8–11). The psalmist, too, portrays the clouds as God's chariot and the winds as God's angels or messengers, while fire and flame are God's servants or ministers (Ps. 104:3–4). *Rûaḥ* can, then, be wind, but we should not take that to mean *mere* wind.

We need look no further for more of this in Scripture than the sixteenth and seventeenth words of the Hebrew Bible: *rûaḥ 'ĕlōhîm*. Right at the beginning of the Bible, these words defy translation. The NRSV translates them as "a wind from God." The NIV translates them as "the Spirit of God." *The Message* reads, "God's Spirit." In the context of creation, a wind from God brooding over the abyss makes perfect sense. In fact, a parallel between darkness and spirit suggests the likelihood that two *material* presences are active prior to creation:

> and darkness   covered   the face of the deep,
> and *rûaḥ* of God swept over the face of the waters.

This first appearance of *rûaḥ* in the Bible is indispensable for a robust understanding of spirit. Understood even as an elemental wind, akin to primeval darkness, this wind is God's *rûaḥ*, like the wind that delivered quail to the famished Israelites in the wilderness. If it is wind, it is *God's* wind. This first appearance also illuminates the strength of ambiguity: spirit is wind, wind is spirit. To divide natural from supernatural, material from spiritual, is to ignore the cue in the first words of Scripture. Wind and spirit are indistinguishable from each other in this first appearance of the word *rûaḥ*.

Wind and spirit *and breath*, in fact, are indistinguishable from one another in these early lines of Scripture. *Rûaḥ* will shortly play an implicit role as the breath of God, who will form powerful words that divide darkness from light, sea from land, night from day: *and God said* (Gen. 1:1–2:4). *Rûaḥ* in its debut is a strange but not accidental alchemy of Spirit (it is explicitly *rûaḥ* of *God*), wind (it spans the waters, just as darkness covers the abyss), and breath (in the next line, God will begin to bring order to the chaos of the abyss with well-spoken words).

Breath

The understanding of *rûaḥ* in the sense of breath occupies many corners of the Jewish Bible. In the first flood, for example, humans and animals with the breath of the spirit of life[4] in them perish under the swells of unruly water (Gen. 7:22).

This understanding of *rûaḥ* runs through the prophets. According to Isaiah, for instance, the messianic ruler will kill the wicked with the *rûaḥ* of his mouth (11:4). God, claims a prophet of the exile, gives breath[5] to people on the earth and spirit to those who walk on it (Isa. 42:5). The prophet of Isaiah 57:16 speaks for God, who promises,

> For I will not continually accuse,
>   nor will I always be angry;
> for then the spirits would grow faint before me,
>   even the breaths[6] I have made.

God's relentless anger would cause human beings to faint, breathless before divine wrath.

The presence of breath permeates the wisdom tradition as well. The author of Lamentations describes the intimacy with which the messiah, the anointed, "the breath of our life,"[7] was held (Lam. 4:20). Job complains that his breath, "my spirit," is loathsome to his wife (Job 19:17).

Elsewhere in the book of Job, *rûaḥ* is breath but not *mere* breath. Job tells his companions to ask the animals, birds, plants, and fish,

---

4. Hebrew, *nišmaṯ-rûaḥ ḥayyîm*.
5. Hebrew, *nəšāmâ*.
6. NRSV "souls;" Hebrew, *ûnəšāmôṯ*.
7. Hebrew, *rûaḥ ʾappênû*.

and they will declare that in God's hand "is the life[8] of every living thing and the *rûaḥ* of every human being" (Job 12:7–10). He then raises the protest that he will have integrity "as long as my breath[9] is in me and the *rûaḥ* of God is in my nostrils" (27:3). This is the bare-bones expression of the spirit in the valley of the shadow of death. Breath is spirit, and spirit is the source of integrity. With a gasp, Job claims that only truthful words will come from his mouth as long as *rûaḥ*, the spirit-breath of God, can roll over his parched tongue.

Job is not alone, surrounded as he is by men who are trying, if unsuccessfully, to wrest meaning from his situation. Job, in agony, grabs hold of a truth that young Elihu, who has stood by and listened impatiently to his elders, claims to grasp as well:

> But truly it is the *rûaḥ* in a mortal,
>> the breath of the Almighty,[10] that makes for
>> understanding.
> It is not the old that are wise,
>> nor the aged that understand what is right. (Job 32:8–9)

Breath is not *mere* breath. Spirit is never *mere* spirit. *Rûaḥ* is not *mere rûaḥ*. The spirit in a mortal is no less than the breath of the Almighty; the spirit-breath in a human being, in other words, does not belong to the mortal but to God. Centuries later, the Jewish author of the Wisdom of Solomon would appeal to the Greek notion of a borrowed soul that has to be given back to God at death (15:7–13). That is not exactly what Elihu means, but there is a baseline truth that my spirit, my breath, my spirit-breath, my *rûaḥ*, is *God's*. It is not *mere* spirit-breath.

Admittedly, Elihu grasps this truth but does not execute it well. He may have the spirit-breath of God in him, producing words that roll over his tongue, but when he speaks, he crushes a battered Job with tactless and thoughtless words (as so often happens in the face of suffering). Elihu is insensitive to the core, hardly wise, and hardly able to understand, as he puts it, what is right. Nonetheless, he reckons,

---

8. Hebrew, *nepeš*.
9. Hebrew, *nišmāṯî*.
10. Hebrew, *wənišmaṯ šadday*.

with Job, that breath is not *mere* breath but a font of wisdom, even if he does not yet know how to tap that wisdom.

With Job, Israelite worshipers preoccupied with praise of God express a tension between the bane of bereavement and the lavishness of life. This concern wriggles its way into Israel's book of worship in two climactic expressions of individual praise:

> I will sing to the LORD *as long as I live*;
>> I will sing praise to my God *while I yet live*. (Ps. 104:33)

> I will praise the LORD *as long as I live*;
>> I will sing praises to my God *while I yet live*. (Ps. 146:2)[11]

Song and praise punctuate these refrains and suggest nothing other than an unabashedly positive affirmation of life. Yet the words *as long as* and *while*, as in Job's protest, hint at the limits of life that circumscribe praise. In light of what we have discovered so far in Israel's stories and wisdom literature, it comes as no surprise that Israel's poetry also expresses the keen awareness that life's end is concurrent with the loss of God's spirit-breath.

Because the shadow of death draped itself heavily over the destinies of countless unnamed Israelite individuals, the first of these psalms contains a poignant glimpse of the power that the spirit was believed to hold. This power was not exclusively in the world of miracles, in the immense power of a Samson or Saul but, even more profoundly, in the wrestling match with death.

For several stanzas of Psalm 104, harmony reigns. The winds are God's messengers. The earth is set firmly on its foundations. Springs and streams satisfy the earth. Cattle eat grass. Humans drink wine. Trees are watered. Birds and goats and storks have suitable homes. The sun and moon mark time. People labor until evening. Ships sail the seas. Even Leviathan sports in the water! God, in the end, can be trusted to provide: "These all look to you to give them their food in due season; when you give to them, they gather it up; when you open

---

11. Though the Hebrew is the same in both poems, NRSV translates the final words of Ps. 104:33 with "while I have being" and the final words of Ps. 146:2 with "all my life long." The portion in italics, which represents my translation, reflects the similarity in Hebrew.

your hand, they are filled with good things" (104:27–28). All is indeed right with the world, leading to untrammeled praise: "May the glory of the LORD endure forever. . . . I will sing to the LORD as long as I live; I will sing praise to my God while I yet live" (104:31a, 33). All is indeed right, except for death, which enters this poem discreetly in the words "as long as I live" and "while I yet live." Praise, even unbounded praise, is bound by death.

Death disrupts and dismays even the animals that have learned to expect good things from God's hand. The poet delicately shapes this ambivalent conviction about the spirit, life, and death through mirror imaging:

> When you hide your *face* [*pānîm*], they are dismayed;
> when you take away their *spirit* [*rûaḥ*], they die
> and return to their dust.
> When you send forth your *spirit* [*rûaḥ*], they are created;
> and you renew the *face* [*pānîm*] of the ground. (Ps.
> 104:29–30, italics added)

Along with powerful poetic symmetry—*pānîm* at the start matches *pānîm* at the end, while *rûaḥ* taken matches *rûaḥ* sent—a concentrated cluster of allusions to the creation and curses of *adam*[12] informs these few lines. This is not surprising, as the psalm in its entirety consists of praise of God as creator, and creation in Genesis is marred quickly, almost immediately, by the possibility (Gen. 2:17) and then the inevitability (3:19) of death.

The poet knows that death is no benign passing from one sphere of existence to another. Death is divine absence—the hiding of God's presence-face.[13] The hiding of God's presence-face in this poem con-

12. Technically, this word should be transliterated *ʾāḏām*, but I've left it *adam* throughout for easier reading.

13. I will use the phrase *presence-face* throughout this book because I do not think either *presence* or *face*, though both are viable translations, captures the resonance of the Hebrew word *pānîm*. *Pānîm* is more than the abstract notion of presence and other than God's face. Think of the intense negotiation between God and Moses at Mt. Sinai, where Moses presses God to accompany Israel. God relents: "My *pānîm* will go with you, and I will give you rest." Moses, still uncertain, seals the deal: "If your *pānîm* will not go, do not carry us up from here" (Exod. 33:14–15). Moses here wants more than a general sense of divine presence and something other than God's

tains a haunting reminiscence of Genesis 3:8, the moment at which "the man and his wife hid themselves from the presence [*pānîm*] of the LORD God among the trees of the garden." Death also portends spiritless or breathless existence. God had, in the beginning, pressed God's face intimately against *adam*'s to breathe life into lifeless dust. Now God's face turns away and takes away the spirit, prompting disintegration into dust and fulfilling the curse of Genesis 3:19: "You are dust, and to dust you shall return."

If the pendulum of Psalm 104 swings toward divine hiddenness and loss of spirit in its reimagining of Genesis, it also swings toward the creative impulse of God. What characterized *adam* in Genesis 2:7 is expanded to encompass the entirety of the animal world. Animals are not merely objects of human hunger but subjects who have a relationship with God. They live in God's presence, God's face; they possess God's spirit; and they return to the dust. What Genesis said about human beings, the poet says about animals as well.

This is not an image of new creation in any simple sense nor the end of one era and the beginning of another. This is rather a realistic image of hope intertwined with the inevitability of despair. What this poet grasps with remarkable acuity is that a life abounding in praise and song is possible within the boundaries of disintegration and death. The poet will sing to the Lord *as long as* he lives; he will sing praise while he *yet* lives. Praise and song persevere despite the inevitability of death. The poet reckons with the tension that exists between death and creation, the suspension of life between the face of God and the face of the earth.

Pivotal to this perception is God's spirit. Its absence brings a world of dismay, of God's hiddenness, of death and dust. Yet its presence brings life, creation, and renewal of the ground. The pendulum does indeed swing in this song between death and life, life and death, but it swings more widely toward life than it does toward death. The spirit

---

face. In the end, Moses's uncertainty is justified, as there is a certain intractability to divine denial. "But," God says, "you cannot see my *pānîm*; for no one shall see me and live" (33:20). In light of biblical texts such as this one, I prefer the combination *presence-face* as a translation to capture the richness of *pānîm*. If you want to learn more about the fascinating conception of God's *pānîm*, you will find a detailed discussion in my book *The Holy Spirit before Christianity* (Waco: Baylor University Press, 2019), 21–25, 167–70nn110–46.

may be taken away, but it will also be given. And the earth will be refreshed along with it. Death—dearth of God's spirit—cannot have the final say; life—creation by God's spirit—comes along to renew the lifeless earth. The poet can sing in the brief span of a lifetime not because he ignores the harsh realities of existence but because he knows that the hiding of God's face in death can be undone, unraveled, by the giving of God's spirit-breath, by which the face of the ground is rehabilitated.

The second of these psalms, this one in praise of God's reign over prisoners and the oppressed, evokes an inescapable but ambiguous association of spirit and death. In this particular psalm, the familiar refrain, "I will praise the LORD as long as I live; I will sing praises to my God while I yet live," leads to the command not to trust in princes. No mortal is reliable; to trust in a son of *adam* is futile because his thoughts or plans, prince though he may be, will die when his spirit goes out of him:

> Put not your trust in princes,
>   in a son of *adam*, in whom there is no help.
> When his *spirit* [*rûaḥ*] departs, he returns to his earth;
>   on that very day his plans perish. (Ps. 146:3–4 alt.)

This portion of the psalm, like Psalm 104, is filled with allusions to the early chapters of the book of Genesis, though with different creative twists. The psalmist puts rulers in their place by referring to them as nothing more than "sons of *adam*." Like the first *adam*, their father, they come from the earth. Further, the phrase *he returns to his earth* recalls Genesis 3:19, though death is personalized in the psalm. It is not *the* earth in general that the prince returns to but *his* own earth, *his* own plot of ground. This is a fascinating detail, particularly in light of Psalm 104:29, in which animals are said to return to *their* dust as well: "When you hide your face, they are dismayed; when you take away their spirit, they die and return to their dust." Death is personal. Deeply personal. Finally, the poet includes the spirit-breath in his description of a prince's death: "When his spirit [*rûaḥ*] departs, he returns to his earth." With this description of death, the psalmist has replaced the original breath of life (*nišmat ḥayyîm*) of Genesis 2:7 with spirit (*rûaḥ*), although the meaning seems to be much the same.

No simple, salubrious portrait of the spirit as a creative and life-inducing element of existence is in this psalm. There is only the negative image of the spirit's withdrawal at the moment of death, of a return to earth, of an immediate destruction of plans. This is due no doubt to the effort of the poet to put princes in their place and to commend a life of trust in God, who reigns, unlike the sons of *adam*, "forever" (Ps. 146:10).[14]

Wind as God's Breath

Whether in Torah, Prophets, or Writings, the spirit can be breath—not necessarily *mere* breath, never simply breath as physical existence but a reservoir of hard-earned and easily forfeited vitality and sagacity, just as wind is not necessarily *mere* wind but a chariot on which God rides with a bird's-eye view of the earth.[15]

The ambiguity of *rûaḥ* emerges at the center of Israel's memory of the exodus in descriptions that could just as easily refer to God's breath or God's wind. A poetic reflection of the escape across the sea from the marauding Egyptians in Exodus 15:8 and 10 describes the event in this way:

> With the spirit-breath [*rûaḥ*] of your nostrils[16] the waters
> were piled up. . . .
> You blew with your spirit-breath [*rûaḥ*], the sea covered
> them.[17]

Rûaḥ must be the wind that caused the waters to divide on either side of the escaping band of slaves. Yet it is not merely wind. It must also be God's breath: what came from God's nose, what God blew.

14. I have devoted an entire chapter of *Fresh Air: The Holy Spirit for an Inspired Life* (Brewster, MA: Paraclete, 2012) to the spirit-breath of God. See pp. 20–41.

15. Often, too, it is said that idols have no breath in them. God possesses what idols do not: *rûaḥ* (e.g., Hab. 2:19; Ps. 135:17).

16. Or anger.

17. This is my translation. NRSV reads: "At the blast of your nostrils the waters piled up. . . . You blew with your wind, the sea covered them."

This intersection of wind and divine breath is apparent elsewhere in the Jewish Scriptures. The prophet of the exile claims that

> The grass withers, the flower fades,
>> when the *rûaḥ* of the LORD blows upon it;
>> surely the people are grass.
> The grass withers, the flower fades;
>> but the word of our God will stand forever. (Isa. 40:7–8)

A scorching wind, of course, causes grass to wither and flowers to fade, but the wind is also God's breath blown over them. This intersection of wind and breath, along with the association with God's word, emerges again in Psalm 147:18:

> He [God] sends out his word, and melts them;
>> he makes his *rûaḥ* blow, and the waters flow.

This psalm, like Isaiah 40:7, understands wind as God's breath blown over the waters; the pairing of *rûaḥ* with God's word makes it clear that the wind that blows is nothing other than God's breath, with which God speaks. So wind and breath are one and the same *rûaḥ*. The breath of God that forms God's word functions as a wind, which withers grass, melts hail, and causes waters to flow. Similarly, in Psalm 33:6–7:

> By the word of the LORD the heavens were made,
>> and all their host by the *rûaḥ* of his mouth.
> He [the LORD] gathered the waters of the sea as in a bottle;
>> he put the deeps in storehouses.

Again, word and *rûaḥ* from God's mouth are the winds that move the waters, holding them in their heavenly treasuries. Psalm 18:15 (MT 18:16) is comparable:

> Then the channels of the sea were seen,
>> and the foundations of the world were laid bare
> at your rebuke, O LORD,
>> at the blast of the *rûaḥ* of your nostrils.[18]

18. Though translated in the NRSV as "blast," the Hebrew reads *nišmat rûaḥ 'appekā*—"the breath of the spirit of your nose." The same phrase occurs in 2 Sam. 22:16.

In this reflection upon Genesis 1:1–2:4, coupled with an allusion to the parting of the sea in Exodus 15:8–10, the breath of the *rûaḥ* of God's nostrils produces the threatening word that causes the waters to part during the creation of channels and land masses. Word and wind are one.

In another reflection on creation, God is said to hang the earth on nothing, bind the water on thick clouds, cover the face of the moon, describe a circle on the face of the waters, rebuke the pillars of heaven, still the sea by God's power, strike down Rahab by God's understanding, and pierce the fleeing serpent with God's hand. In this context, it is said that by God's *rûaḥ* "the heavens were made fair" (Job 26:7–13, esp. 13). In such a context, which catalogs God's activities, this *rûaḥ* is not only wind but the breath God blows in the form of creative wind. God hangs, binds, covers, rebukes, stills, strikes down, pierces, and blows *rûaḥ* into the heavens to make them beautiful.

Arguably the most dazzling fusion of wind, breath, and spirit—all of them *rûaḥ* in Hebrew—occurs in Ezekiel's grand vision of very many, very dry bones. The vision begins once the Lord, with a heavy hand on Ezekiel, brings him to rest by (or in) the *rûaḥ* of the Lord in a valley. At first blush, the *rûaḥ* looks like an actual wind that transports Ezekiel to a distant valley: "The hand of the LORD came upon me, and he brought me out by the *rûaḥ* of the LORD and set me down in the middle of a valley; it was full of bones" (Ezek. 37:1). This is probably not an actual wind. The advent of this *rûaḥ* likely signals a visionary experience that recalls Ezekiel's first vision, when *rûaḥ* lifted him up in the context of his initial calling:

> Then the *rûaḥ* lifted me up, and as the glory of the LORD rose from its place, I heard behind me the sound of loud rumbling. . . . The *rûaḥ* lifted me up and bore me away; I went in bitterness in the heat of my *rûaḥ*, the hand of the LORD being strong upon me. I came to the exiles at Tel-abib, who lived by the river Chebar. And I sat there among them, stunned, for seven days. (Ezek. 3:12, 14–15)

Ezekiel's experience of *rûaḥ* is visionary rather than physical. The beginning of the book makes this crystal clear: "In the thirtieth year, in the fourth month, on the fifth day of the month, as I was among the exiles by the river Chebar, the heavens were opened, and *I saw visions of God*" (1:1).

Ezekiel's other experiences of *rûaḥ* are also visionary. Ezekiel spots a human-looking figure with fire below its waist and gleaming amber above.

> It stretched out the form of a hand, and took me by a lock of my head; and the *rûaḥ* lifted me up between earth and heaven, and brought me *in visions of* God to Jerusalem, to the entrance of the gateway of the inner court that faces north, to the seat of the image of jealousy, which provokes to jealousy. And the glory of the God of Israel was there, like *the vision* that I had seen in the valley. (Ezek. 8:3–4, italics added)

Ezekiel's subsequent experience is visionary as well: "The *rûaḥ* lifted me up and brought me to the east gate of the house of the LORD, which faces east" (11:1). This experience concludes, "The *rûaḥ* lifted me up and brought me *in a vision* by the *rûaḥ* of God into Chaldea, to the exiles. Then *the vision* that I had seen left me" (11:24). The work of the *rûaḥ* in this conclusion is visionary transport. What the rest of the book of Ezekiel means for Ezekiel 37:1 should be clear: Ezekiel's experience of *rûaḥ* is visionary rather than physical. Nevertheless, the ambiguity of Ezekiel's language blurs the border between physical and visionary; this is certainly not the language of body versus spirit. Recall Ezekiel's first experience, when he went "in bitterness in the heat of my *rûaḥ*, the hand of the LORD being strong upon me" (3:14). *Rûaḥ* may not be an actual wind, but *rûaḥ* does create an experience that is upsetting, unnerving, and transporting.

This initial ambiguity is only the start of the vision of very many, very dry bones coming back to life. In this strange and riveting vision, Ezekiel is instructed to prophesy to the bones: "I [God] will cause *rûaḥ* to enter you, and you shall live" (Ezek. 37:5). The bones rattle; sinews and flesh grow. But there is no *rûaḥ* in the bones. So again, Ezekiel is instructed, "Prophesy to the *rûaḥ* . . . : 'Come, *rûaḥ*, from the four *rûḥôt*.'" As a result, "*rûaḥ* entered them," and the bones "came to life and stood up on their feet—a vast army" (37:9–10). Here, in a magnificent vision of a revitalized nation, ambiguity strains to the breaking point: *rûaḥ* as *breath* enters into the bones only when it comes from the four *rûḥôt*, the four *winds* at the corners of the earth. Wind is breath. Breath is wind. All of this, begun when *rûaḥ* transported Ezekiel in a vision to a valley of very many, very dry bones, is life beyond limits, hope beyond dreams.

The result is a luscious promise: "I will put my *rûaḥ* within you, and you shall live, and I will place you on your own soil; then you shall know that I, the LORD, have spoken and will act, says the LORD" (Ezek. 37:14). The intensity of this promise is evident only in light of the ambiguity of *rûaḥ*. Though translators are forced to opt for *spirit* or *Spirit* in this final reference to *rûaḥ*, the promise gains traction only in view of the reality that God had filled the bones with *rûaḥ* when the winds, the four *rûḥôt*, converged on a valley of very many, very dry bones. *Breath. Winds. Spirit.* What God promises, God has already accomplished—except to bring those bodies back to the promised land from exile in Babylon.

It is impossible to capture in English translation the drama of the original Hebrew, where all three English words—*breath*, *wind*, and *spirit*—are one: *rûaḥ*. Ezekiel repeats this word in order to emphasize that the one and only *rûaḥ* of God inspires the resurrection of Israel—a resurrection that is at once a creation like *adam*'s (*rûaḥ* as breath), a rush of vitality (*rûaḥ* as winds), and a promise of fidelity in their homeland (*rûaḥ* as life-giving spirit). The beating of the drum of *rûaḥ* is simultaneously personal, cosmic, and national; to subdivide this word, as translators are compelled to do, is to lose the power of ambiguity, by which Ezekiel piles up the connotations of *rûaḥ* to pound resurrection into Israel's deadened psyche.

The intimate connection between God's breath and wind, then, came to a resplendent climax in the experience of Ezekiel, during the ominous decade following the deportation of Judah's leaders in 597 BCE, followed by the wholesale destruction of Jerusalem in 587 BCE. When hope was at its lowest ebb and Israel chanted the threnody, "Our bones are dried up, and our hope is lost; we are cut off completely" (Ezek. 37:11), Ezekiel imagined the highest intensification in Israelite literature of *rûaḥ* as breath, wind, and the source of national restoration. Not affluence and ease but communal crisis yielded literature of unsurpassed hope in the power and potential of God's *rûaḥ* to breathe new life into a defeated and dislocated community.[19]

19. If you would like to learn more about this *rûaḥ* in Ezekiel's vision, you will find a scholarly analysis in my *Filled with the Spirit* (Grand Rapids: Eerdmans, 2009), 87–103, 202–17, as well as a more popular discussion in my *Fresh Air*, 141–65.

2

Spirit Coming Upon

Before reading this chapter, explore these texts:

>> Numbers 24:1–9
>> Judges 3:9–12
>> Judges 6:33–35
>> Judges 11:29–33
>> Judges 13:24–25; 14:1–9, 15–20; 15:14–17
>> 1 Samuel 10:1–8; 11:1–11; 16:13–23; 19:18–24
>> 1 Chronicles 12:16–18
>> 2 Chronicles 15:1–7
>> 2 Chronicles 20:13–17
>> 2 Chronicles 24:20–22

The strange notion of *rûaḥ* in the Hebrew Scriptures shatters taxonomies, leaving us to ask mistakenly, "Is *rûaḥ* wind? Breath? Spirit? Or spirit?" In particular, *rûaḥ* causes tidy dichotomies to splinter, neat categories to fragment. In Israelite antiquity, a wind from the sea carrying quail might be every bit as much—or more—divine as the power that prompts elders to prophesy. *Rûaḥ* rolling over the tongue of a disconsolate man on an ash heap may evoke as much—or more—wisdom than a surprise onslaught of spirit. In short, familiar distinctions between divine and human, comfortable boundaries between sacred and profane, accustomed borders between spiritual and material, evaporate in the presence of *rûaḥ*.

The distinction between the personal and political also vanishes. The Hebrew Scriptures do not allow the spirit to be sequestered within the secure confines of the individual or the relatively safe space of the church. When it comes to *rûaḥ*, private yields to public. The profane, rather than the sacred, is the sphere of the spirit's influence.

This is apparent right at the start, when the *rûaḥ* of God hovers over the cosmic abyss (Gen. 1:1–2); when, in the flood, drowning humans and animals alike possess the breath of the spirit of life (6:17; 7:15, 22); when, in the story of Joseph, an Egyptian pharaoh—a foreign ruler whose empire was unparalleled at the time—recognizes the *rûaḥ* of God in Joseph (41:38). The book of Genesis, which contains our first clues to the world of the spirit, positions the *rûaḥ* above the abyss, in the throats of both human and animal, and in Joseph, whose wisdom is recognized by an alien ruler. There is nothing in the book of Genesis to suggest that the spirit is only *spiritual*, that its sphere of influence lies exclusively within the *individual*, or that discernment of matters related to the spirit is *ecclesial*, belonging solely to a community of faith or a church of some sort. Not a pious but a profane, pagan ruler has the wherewithal to acknowledge the *rûaḥ* in Joseph.

The spirit, in short, was not yet tame in the annals of Israelite literature. Absent the creeds, long before Christians annexed philosophy to grasp the nature of the spirit, Israel told stories of a mysterious presence that prompted remarkable feats in the public sphere. The comfortable constraints of later generations were not yet in place; this is untamed wilderness. Not gardens but forests. Not fields but plains.

Balaam

This may be why the memories of the judges, upon whom the spirit came in power so that they could liberate Israel, are among the oldest memories of the spirit in the Jewish Bible. Yet even before the powerful *rûaḥ* rushed upon these Israelite judges, as the story is told, the first person on whom the spirit comes, in a bizarre twist, is not Israelite at all.[1]

In a peculiar story toward the tail end of the book of Numbers, which recounts Israel's plodding but relentless movement toward the promised land, Israel is poised to enter Canaan. They are now east of the Jordan River in the region of Moab, where Moab's king, Balak, is anxious because of what he heard about the Israelites as they made their way to Moab. So Balak sends his messengers, money for divination in hand, to Balaam, a Mesopotamian seer who hails from the Fertile Crescent. This is a dire ploy, but Balak knows that "whomever you [Balaam] bless is blessed, and whomever you curse is cursed" (Num. 22:6). This, of course, is a sinister twist on the promise God made time and again to Israel's ancestor Jacob: whoever blessed Israel would be blessed; whoever cursed Israel would be cursed (Gen. 27:29).

After much persuasion on the part of Balak's emissaries, Balaam heads to Moab, but his donkey sees an angel blocking the way. God is displeased. After a serious confrontation with the donkey, Balaam realizes that he cannot offer curse-for-hire; he must, rather, speak the truth. When Balaam and Balak set up seven altars, presumably for the purpose of divination (analyzing the animals' organs or the patterns in the sacrificial smoke), what Balaam says does not curse Israel. So he sets up another seven altars elsewhere, only to come to the same conclusion. Then he sets up a third set of altars. This time, however, "Balaam saw that it pleased the LORD to bless Israel, so he did not go, as at other times, to look for omens, but set his face toward the wilderness. Balaam looked up and saw Israel camping tribe by tribe. Then the *rûaḥ* of God came upon him, and he uttered his oracle, saying . . ." (Num. 24:1–3).[2]

---

1. Others earlier in the biblical story are said to be wise and skilled because they are filled with *rûaḥ*: Joseph (Gen. 41:38), the artisans responsible for the tabernacle (Exod. 28:3), and their esteemed leaders, Bezalel and Oholiab (Exod. 31:1–6; 35:30–36:7). These will be discussed in chap. 6. In contrast to such filling, the spirit comes *upon* Balaam.

2. The translation "came upon him" may be too strong. The verb, rather, is "to be": the spirit of God *was* upon him. It could even be argued that the translation

This turn of events, this transformation of Balaam, whether superficial or authentic, was fundamental to Israel's understanding of inspiration. The world of the spirit is *not* open to manipulation. Only *after* Balaam chooses not to look for omens does the *rûaḥ* of God inspire his oracle. Israel was adamant early on about this point. The eighth-century prophet Micah drew a radical distinction between his own claim to the spirit and the claims of other prophets, who adopted the ruse of dreams and divination to discover a word pleasing to the king. Those prophets, Micah knew, would be met with darkness and disgrace (Mic. 3:1–8). The book of Deuteronomy, too, sees a chasm between divination, consulting the dead, and the practice of incubation (a ritual aimed at receiving revelation through dreams) and the world of faith (Deut. 18:9–14).

This point is inescapable: the *rûaḥ* of God cannot be manipulated by ritual or routine. Still another surprise in this story may be that the spirit does not actually transform Balaam. Balaam had already realized that God would not bless or curse Israel through ill-gotten omens *before* the *rûaḥ* came upon him: "Balaam saw that it pleased the LORD to bless Israel, so he did not go, as at other times, to look for omens, but set his face toward the wilderness." This is an important detail. Balaam *already* underwent a change of heart by the time "the *rûaḥ* of God came upon him, and he uttered his oracle." The spirit was not upon Balaam in order to work *against* the wicked wiles of a non-Israelite. On the contrary—and this may be one of many surprises in the Old Testament—the spirit came upon a receptive non-Israelite seer, an outsider, someone not included among the chosen nation.[3]

One more point worth noting is that Balaam's experience is a fusion of vision and speech. What he sees is what he says. What he

---

should read, "Now the spirit of God had been upon him, so he lifted this oracle and said . . ." Earlier in the story God put a word in his mouth (Num. 23:5, 16); this was the sign of a prophet, although the spirit is not mentioned until Num. 24:2.

3. The result of the spirit's presence, at first blush, seems to be a *spoken* oracle. This may be the case, but the substance of what Balaam communicates is a *vision*:

> The oracle of Balaam son of Beor,
>   the oracle of the man whose eye is clear [or closed],
> the oracle of one who hears the words of God,
>   who sees the vision of the Almighty,
>   who falls down, but with eyes uncovered. (Num. 24:3–4)

says, further, is not particularly original; his oracle is rich with similes that sound like the Song of Songs, although they are aimed not at a lover but at Israel. The oracle ends predictably, reminiscent of the promise made to Abraham and Sarah, Isaac and Rebekah, Jacob, Leah, and Rachel: "Blessed is everyone who blesses you, and cursed is everyone who curses you" (Num. 24:9). The spirit does not, in other words, inspire new language and a novel vision. The spirit simply allows Balaam to see reality as it is rather than as he had erroneously perceived it. What the spirit inspires in Balaam is not a framework for the future, an unprecedented prediction, a sensational glimpse of the world to come, but a clarity about reality as God sees it. Such clarity, such a course correction, is the quintessential work of the spirit. Such clarity is the essence of prophecy.

Judges

Balaam is a blip in Israel's memory, even if the story occupies a full three chapters. The temporary presence of the spirit on Israel's judges, however, is not a blip; it occurs a half dozen times throughout the book of Judges. The paradigm for liberation occurs in a brief sketch of the first judge:

> But when the Israelites cried out to the LORD, the LORD raised up a deliverer for the Israelites, who delivered them, Othniel son of Kenaz, Caleb's younger brother. The spirit of the LORD came upon him, and he judged Israel; he went out to war, and the LORD gave King Cushan-rishathaim of Aram into his hand; and his hand prevailed over Cushan-rishathaim. So the land had rest forty years. Then Othniel son of Kenaz died. The Israelites again did what was evil in the sight of the LORD; and the LORD strengthened King Eglon of Moab against Israel, because they had done what was evil in the sight of the LORD. (Judg. 3:9–12)

This sketch sets the pattern for many of the judges to come: Israel is oppressed by nearby nations; Israel cries out; a deliverer arises; the spirit comes upon the judge; the judge delivers Israel; Israel has peace; Israel sins and is again oppressed, which begins the cycle afresh. Slight variations characterize this pattern. The spirit *is upon* Othniel and Jephthah (Judg. 3:10; 11:29). The spirit *clothes* Gideon (6:34). The spirit *rushes upon* Samson (14:6, 19; 15:14). But the pattern remains the same.

The new and disturbing element in Judges is the possible association of the spirit with war. Othniel, Gideon, Jephthah, and Samson are, after all, leaders who liberate their people. To escape this association, it can be argued that the judges were not about the matter of war but the matter of reestablishing fragmented communal solidarity. "Even the early experiences of God's Spirit are *experiences of how a new beginning is made toward restoring the community of God's people.* They are *experiences of the forgiveness of sins, of the raising up of the 'crushed and oppressed,'* and of the renewal of the *forces of life.*"[4] There is truth in this perspective. When the spirit clothes Gideon, he gathers the people together (Judg. 6:34). When the spirit comes upon Jephthah, he passes through Gilead and Manasseh to gather the people (11:29). The spirit first stirs in Samson not when he is on the cusp of wholesale slaughter but as he wanders alone through the circle of his ancestors, in his family's burial ground (13:25).

The weight of Judges, however, also rests heavily upon a link between the spirit and the specter of violence. Othniel's only recorded actions are to judge Israel and to lead them successfully into battle.

Gideon finds himself shortly in the company of all the troops that were with him (Judg. 7:2). When these troops muster for battle later, they do not fight at all—a point that would support the view that the spirit restores solidarity. They outmaneuver their opponents when they descend upon the Midianite camp with trumpets blaring, lamps burning, and voices shouting; even still, though the Israelites avoid killing of any sort, their actions impel the Midianites to destroy one another. The spirit leads Gideon ultimately to the avoidance of war but not to the avoidance of death.

Jephthah, too, may not yet have entered battle, but he undertakes his journey through Gilead and Manasseh to muster the troops ahead of battle with the Ammonites. The spirit may be one step away from battle, but that step is inevitably in the direction of war.

4. Michael Welker, *God the Spirit* (Minneapolis: Fortress, 1994), 65 (italics original).

When the spirit rushed upon Samson for a first time, he tore apart a lion (Judg. 14:6). A second time, "he went down to Ashkelon" and "killed thirty men" (14:19). A third time, the spirit gave him superhuman strength, causing what bound him to melt; immediately he found the fresh jawbone of a donkey and killed a thousand men with it (15:14–15). These episodes seem to confirm the connection between the spirit and violence.

Despite this impression, there may be a way to interpret the stories of Samson without attributing violence to the spirit. It may be, as the story is told, that the spirit actually attempts to keep Samson from becoming violent. This interpretation hinges upon Samson's first experience of the spirit, in which the spirit troubles or stirs him while he wanders between Zorah and Eshtaol (Judg. 13:25).[5] This is not at all suitable for someone like Samson, who has taken a Nazirite vow. As a Nazirite, Samson must not touch a corpse.[6] Yet there he is, wandering between Zorah and Eshtaol in his family burial ground, where the tomb of his father Manoah can be found (16:31). Why the spirit should stir or trouble him is not at all clear. Perhaps it is to stir or trouble Samson so that he will *not* wander there—in other words, to *prevent* Samson from contact with corpses, which would break his Nazirite vow.

5. Hebrew, *wattāḥel rûaḥ yhwh ləpaʿămô*.
6. The laws for Nazirites, which are found in Num. 6, illuminate the story of Samson:

> The LORD spoke to Moses, saying: Speak to the Israelites and say to them: When either men or women make a special vow, the vow of a nazirite, to separate themselves to the LORD, they shall separate themselves from wine and strong drink; they shall drink no wine vinegar or other vinegar, and shall not drink any grape juice or eat grapes, fresh or dried. All their days as nazirites they shall eat nothing that is produced by the grapevine, not even the seeds or the skins.
>
> All the days of their nazirite vow no razor shall come upon the head; until the time is completed for which they separate themselves to the LORD, they shall be holy; they shall let the locks of the head grow long.
>
> All the days that they separate themselves to the LORD they shall not go near a corpse. Even if their father or mother, brother or sister, should die, they may not defile themselves; because their consecration to God is upon the head. All their days as nazirites they are holy to the LORD. (Num. 6:1–8)

The laws continue, but these are particularly illuminating for the story of Samson, who lived with apparent disregard for his status as a Nazirite.

From this vantage point, in which the spirit attempts to prevent Samson from violating his vow, we can perhaps view the next three instances as attempts by the spirit to keep Samson from doing violent feats that would violate his vow. When the spirit first comes upon him, it does so to prevent him from killing a lion; he does anyway. Later, in Ashkelon, the spirit comes to prevent him from killing others; he kills thirty anyway. In the third instance, the spirit releases him from the ropes that bind him *in order to escape*, but instead Samson kills a thousand men with the fresh jawbone of a donkey. In each instance, then, the spirit does not come upon Samson to inspire him to kill his enemies; the spirit comes instead, in light of his first experience, to preserve his Nazirite vow. In each instance, Samson resists the spirit, instead acting cavalierly, failing to respond to the rush of the spirit, and failing, consequently, to obey his vow. Ultimately, he brings death to his enemies only by dying himself. Utter tragedy.

There are ways, then, to untangle the spirit from violence in the book of Judges, such as seeing the spirit as the instigator of solidarity for the oppressed or as the power to preserve a vow. Still, the association of the spirit with some sort of violence in these stories is hard to avoid. Whatever we may say about the possible link between the spirit and violence, we can say with certainty that the book of Judges does *not* espouse a universal association between the spirit and violence. The premise of the book of Judges is that God raises liberators only when Israel, oppressed by foreign powers, cries for help—not unlike their ancestors in Egypt, whose cry precipitated a good deal of violence against the Egyptians. If there is an association between the spirit and violence, such violence is only toward dominant nations or empires that actively oppress the Israelites and only on behalf of terribly oppressed people.

Compare these stories in the book of Judges with those that circulate around the apex of Israelite power. In stories of Israel's dominance, such as those that cluster around the reign of Solomon, the spirit is conspicuously absent. In stories that pit prophet against king, such as those that feature Elijah, Elisha, and Micaiah ben Imlah (e.g., 1 Kings 18:12; 22:1–38), the spirit is conspicuous only among prophets who oppose the powerful. In stories that accentuate Israel's vulnerability and fragility, such as those that cluster around the judges, the spirit is conspicuously present in liberation from oppression. The possible association of the spirit with violence, therefore, must be conditioned by the existence of oppression—unequivocal, inescapable oppression such as the Israelites experienced—when solidarity cannot be restored by any other means; violence is a last resort by which the poor are liberated, the final gasp for salvation through leadership in battle against merciless oppressors.

Even then, the pattern is not even or readily extendable. Othniel and Jephthah appear to head into battle. Gideon avoids battle through a brilliant strategy that pits the Midianites against one another. And Samson fights alone against the Philistines; no other foot soldier plays a role.

Troubling is the only way to characterize the possible association of the spirit with liberation in the book of Judges. Yet this troubling dimension rises to the surface because the work of God—and God's spirit—in the work of liberation is ambiguous. Coercion, cruelty, and brutality are rarely broken by persuasion and détente. If the spirit is to be active *in the world*, not just in individuals or the church or the safety of some spiritual realm tucked neatly away from the fray of human history, then the spirit, according to the book of Judges, equips leaders to engage in violent means of liberation.

Or perhaps not. Perhaps the book of Judges preserves the memories of a period in which, as the codicil puts it, everyone did what was right in his or her own eyes because there was no king in Israel (Judg. 21:25). It was an era of anarchy, of generals murdered with tent pegs by women like Jael (Judg. 4–5), of Nazirite vows disregarded by men like Samson, of silly vows made by men like Jephthah (Judg. 11–12), of treachery executed on women like the Levite's concubine (Judg. 19). Perhaps we should *not* extrapolate from these appearances of the spirit a pattern of inspiration. Perhaps this was an era that need not—*must* not—be repeated. Perhaps that, too, is a lesson to be taken from this book of terribly flawed heroes, tyrannical oppressors, and tawdry, terrifying acts of liberation.

Samuel

In the course of time, according to the biblical narrative, intermittent rule by judges gives way to permanent rule by kings, and the life of the seer Samuel marks the transition from judges to kings. The experience of Saul, Israel's first king, begins in a storied way, when Samuel anoints him to be king, predicting, "Then the spirit of the LORD will possess you, and you will *prophesy*[7] along with them and be turned into a different person" (1 Sam. 10:6). Something has changed in the transition from judges to king. There is now not the slightest indication that the change in Saul will be ephemeral. The formula "was upon" or "rushed upon" no longer introduces, as it did in Numbers and Judges, a temporary state. Saul's transformation will be as permanent as his reign.

Saul's transformation is marked by prophesying: "As they traveled from there to Gibeah, a band of prophets met him; and the spirit of God rushed upon him, and he prophesied[8] among them" (1 Sam. 10:10, my translation). Whatever prophesying entails, Saul's experience is prompted by his encounter with a community of prophets, who approach him with musical instruments. Saul's is not a secluded experience of the spirit, nor is it exceptional—something reserved only for kings—in comparison with the band of prophets. On the contrary, Saul acts so much like the prophets that bystanders wonder whether he too is a prophet. It even became a proverb in Israel: "Is Saul also among the prophets?" (10:11).[9]

Saul's next experience of the spirit looks like a flashback to the judges. Told of a plot that would lead to the gouging out of Israel's eyes, "the spirit of God came upon Saul[10] when he heard these words,

---

7. Hebrew *wəhitnabbîṯā*; NRSV "be in a prophetic frenzy."

8. Hebrew, *wayyitnabbē'*.

9. The next instance of prophesying took place, however, when "an evil spirit from God rushed upon Saul, and he prophesied [NRSV "raved"] within his house while David was playing the lyre, as he did day by day. Saul had his spear in his hand" (1 Sam. 18:10). This apparent loss of control would become murderous in the next instance: "Then an evil spirit from the LORD came upon Saul, as he sat in his house with his spear in his hand, while David was playing music" (19:9). The utter loss of control is apparent in the final references in the story to prophesying, when Saul sent messengers to capture David: "When they saw the company of the prophets prophesying, with Samuel standing in charge of them, the spirit of God came upon the messengers of Saul, and they also prophesied" (19:20 alt.). This happened again to two other groups whom Saul sent subsequently. Finally, Saul himself went to capture David but ended up taking off his clothes and lying naked all day and night. The narrator concludes, with apparent irony, "Therefore it is said, 'Is Saul also among the prophets?'" (19:24).

10. I have omitted from the NRSV translation the words *in power*, which are superfluous.

and his anger was greatly kindled. He took a yoke of oxen, and cut them in pieces and sent them throughout all the territory of Israel by messengers, saying, 'Whoever does not come out after Saul and Samuel, so shall it be done to his oxen!' Then the dread of the LORD fell upon the people, and they came out as one" (1 Sam. 11:6–7). Like Samson's, Saul's is hardly a peaceable reaction to the spirit's presence; he responds by issuing an ultimatum to which 370,000 troops respond by gathering for battle. Like Samson, Saul is—or soon will be—an ambiguous character who ignores his responsibilities in an effort to obtain what is not his; in Saul's case, this means taking illicit spoils of battle. And, like Samson, Saul seems bent upon self-destruction.

Therefore, the spirit leaves Saul. When his sins add up to a loss of kingship, the spirit comes permanently upon his successor: "the spirit of the LORD rushed upon David *from that day forward*" (1 Sam. 16:13 alt.). This transference of power suggests a shift in perspective. While judges rose up at moments of crisis, kings were expected to rule until their death—"from that day forward." Judges received the spirit regardless of conspicuous flaws; Saul lost the spirit because of his flaws.

The lesson of Judges was unavoidable. The spirit was active, whether violently or not, in the liberation of an oppressed Israel. When the spirit pressed upon its leaders, the troops were mustered (Gideon; Jephthah), and oppressors ended up powerless (Samson).

Yet this does not imply that Israel's inspired liberators were people of impeccable integrity. Gideon's opening conversation with the angel reveals a cowardly man who threshed grain in a wine pit, where the wind that was needed for threshing could not blow. He was hiding—not threshing. Gideon demanded a sign more than once from the angelic messenger and tore down an idol's altar only in the dark of night (Judg. 6:1–33). Even after he had been clothed in the spirit and defeated the Midianites, Gideon made an egregious error by collecting gold, making an ephod—an image of sorts—of it, and putting it in his hometown, where "all Israel prostituted themselves to it" and "it became a snare to Gideon and to his family" (Judg. 8:27). Later in the story of the judges, Jephthah made an ill-advised and entirely superfluous vow that brought the unnecessary weight of heavy grief when his daughter was the one to emerge from his home (Judg.

11–12). And Samson proved to be a rough-and-tumble womanizer whose wild actions occupied the outskirts of what might be deemed healthy (Judg. 13–16). The judges evince cowardice, scheming, and a disregard for their respective obligations. Yet in none of these cases do egregious character flaws block the advent of the spirit and liberation from oppressors. In none does the spirit withdraw due to a defect. In Saul's case, on the other hand, the spirit leaves him and rushes upon David "from that day forward."

What follows for Saul is one disaster after another, not least Saul's susceptibility to an evil spirit. In a story full of oddities, perhaps the oddest element of all is the uncanny resemblance between the spirit of God and this evil spirit. Right from the start, the departure of God's spirit is marked by the advent of an evil spirit, which repeatedly torments Saul:

> Then Samuel took the horn of oil, and anointed him in the presence of his brothers; and the spirit of the LORD rushed upon David from that day forward. . . . Now the spirit of the LORD departed from Saul, and an evil spirit from the LORD tormented him. And Saul's servants said to him, "See now, an evil spirit from God is tormenting you. Let our lord now command the servants who attend you to look for someone who is skillful in playing the lyre; and when the evil spirit from God is upon you, he will play it, and you will feel better." (1 Sam. 16:13–16 alt.)

> And whenever the evil spirit from God came upon Saul, David took the lyre and played it with his hand, and Saul would be relieved and feel better, and the evil spirit would depart from [upon] him. (1 Sam. 16:23)

> The next day an evil spirit from God rushed upon [toward] Saul, and he prophesied within his house, while David was playing the lyre, as he did day by day. Saul had his spear in his hand. (1 Sam. 18:10 alt.)

> Then an evil spirit from the LORD came upon Saul, as he sat in his house with his spear in his hand, while David was playing music. (1 Sam. 19:9)

The similarities between the spirit of God and an evil spirit in the story of Saul are stunning, puzzling, and inescapable. Both spirits are called a *spirit of God*.[11] Both *rush upon* or *are upon* Saul.[12] Both *depart* from Saul.[13]

The similarities are so striking, in fact, that Saul's final experience of the spirit and prophesying, which mirrors the first (1 Sam. 10:6, 10; 19:20, 23–24), may be due not to the good spirit but to an evil spirit from God.[14] The good spirit of God that had transformed him into another person left him and rushed instead upon David; now the evil spirit of God incapacitates him in an experience that mirrors—or mocks—his first experience of the spirit.[15] Saul meets a community of prophets, as at first, and prophesies, as at first, in some sort of communal ecstasy. This time, however, at the end of a tragic reign, Saul lies naked on the ground overnight. This element of his experience is new.

In an appalling twist, Saul's rise and demise may be marked by unusually similar—but sadly different—experiences. Whether he is inspired by a good or evil spirit—ultimately, we probably cannot say—his final experience of a spirit is marred by vulnerability and vulgarity. And troubling though this may be, both spirits lie within the purview of God, who sends both.

11. 1 Sam. 10:10; 11:6; 16:15, 16, 23a; 18:10; 19:20, 23. Or "spirit of Yahweh" in 10:6; 16:13, 14a (see 14b); 19:9.

12. 1 Sam. 10:6, 10; 11:6; 16:13; 18:10.

13. 1 Sam. 16:14, 23b.

14. 1 Sam. 10:6, 10 (see v. 13); 18:10; 19:20, 23.

15. There are a few compelling reasons to suggest that the spirit from God in 1 Sam. 19 is an *evil* spirit. First, Saul's prophesying accompanies his transformation into another person (1 Sam. 10:6), but in the later event, such prophesying issues in Saul's spending the night in the undignified state of nakedness (19:24). Second, the instance of Saul's "prophesying" that immediately precedes this final experience of prophesying took place when the *evil* spirit of God rushed upon him (18:10). Third, the familiar idiom employed to describe the spirit's presence in 19:19–23, "was upon," occurs otherwise in these stories only of the *evil* spirit (16:16, 23; 19:9). Fourth, each of the seven prior references, from 16:14 to 19:9, is to the *evil* spirit, and its presence is so established that in 16:23 it can be described simply as "spirit of God," without the adjective *evil*. There is no need, from a narrative standpoint, to reintroduce the good spirit when only the evil spirit has been present, especially since the spirit in 1 Sam. 19 causes Saul to lie naked throughout the night. Fifth, the appearance in 1 Sam. 19 of the evil rather than good spirit of God accentuates, by means of a pointed contrast with 1 Sam. 10, the irony of Saul's rise and demise: although Saul prophesies both at the beginning and end of his reign, the source and quality of his experiences are as different as night and day.

This is a baffling story rooted in the promise and demise of a man who, unwittingly perhaps, would be king. In this story, old wine is poured into new wineskins. Traditional formulas known from the book of Judges—the spirit *was upon* Saul—become attached to the evil spirit. The coming of the spirit upon David, too, breaks new ground: the rushing of the spirit, which signaled a *temporary* experience for the likes of Othniel, Gideon, Jephthah, and Samson, brings the spirit to David *from that day forward*. The formulas survive but with fresh associations, as the ominous and ambiguous character of inspiration meets the dubious figure of Saul.

There is a certain inescapable authenticity in the story of Saul. In the public realm, where politics and piety meet, distinguishing between good and evil becomes difficult. Saul's first and last experiences of prophesying by the spirit look nearly alike—except that, in the first instance, a good spirit of God inspires, and in the second, an evil spirit of God arouses him. If a good and an evil spirit can produce nearly the same effects—the operative word here is *nearly*—there is then an urgent need to look, not cursorily but closely, at claims to the spirit. Saul's story raises the specter of discernment, especially when the spirit is believed to operate in the opacity of the political realm, to which equity and tyranny have equal claims.[16]

Inspired Figures in 1–2 Chronicles

The image of the spirit coming as an onslaught of power, though vivid and memorable, lay dormant until the Persian era (after 539 BCE), when it emerged, surprisingly enough, in books whose very names testify to an eye for detail and a penchant for order—what might at first blush seem to be the opposite of inspiration. The au-

16. Despite a difference in wording—and meaning, perhaps—the association of spirit with prophesying in the story of Saul is similar to Ezek. 11:5. In an uncharacteristically brief recollection, Ezekiel recalls how the spirit "fell upon" (the Hebrew root, *npl*, is unlike other verbs) him immediately after he was commanded to prophesy. This claim is too laconic to determine if the story of Saul influenced Ezekiel's claim. There is, as well, one significant difference: it is not apparent whether Saul said anything when he prophesied, while all Ezekiel does in this instance is to speak. Whether or not it draws from the story of Saul, Ezekiel's claim does anticipate a development in 1–2 Chronicles, where individuals upon whom the spirit comes speak prophetic words.

thors of 1–2 Chronicles revised much of what had already appeared in the books of 1–2 Samuel and 1–2 Kings. Those books had explained why the Northern Kingdom, Israel, had fallen to Assyria in 722 BCE and the Southern Kingdom, Judah, to Babylon in 587 BCE. The books of 1–2 Chronicles revise those stories toward a different end: to provide a template for restoration and rebuilding during the centuries after the end of exile in 539 BCE. While 1–2 Samuel and 1–2 Kings look back to come to grips with failure, 1–2 Chronicles retell those stories to ensure success in the years ahead. In this revision, new figures appear that did not play any role in 1–2 Samuel and 1–2 Kings. To four of them—Amasai, Azariah, Jahaziel, and Zechariah—the spirit comes. In stories about all four, a governing theme emerges: the taut connection between the spirit and learning in the service of political expediency.[17]

The first is "Amasai, chief of the Thirty," a group of legendary warriors (1 Chron. 12:18; MT 12:19). When the spirit clothed Amasai, as it had Gideon, Amasai did not prepare for battle, contrary to what the stories of Gideon and Amasai's own leadership in the Thirty might lead us to expect. Instead, this chief warrior lifted his voice rather than his weapon and waxed poetic in support of David: "We are yours, O David; and with you, O son of Jesse! Peace, peace to you, and peace to the one who helps you! For your God is the one who helps you." Success was immediate: "David received them, and made them officers of his troops" (12:18; MT 12:19). There is no surprise in this success. Amasai's poetry is hard-won political rhetoric that subtly but unmistakably represents a pledge of loyalty to David. Just the pair "David" and "son of Jesse" recalls a time when a wicked Nabal had refused, during the reign of Saul, to give food to David's men (1 Sam. 25:10). This time, Amasai pairs "David" with "son of Jesse" but without a hint of disloyalty. Amasai then pronounces "peace" three times upon David and the one who helps him. Even his choice of the words "your God" rather than the traditional "God of our ancestors" is a rhetorical bow to David and David's God (1 Chron. 12:18; MT 12:19). In this poetic snippet,

17. For a little more detail on these figures, esp. Jahaziel, see the discussion in my *Inspired: The Holy Spirit and the Mind of Faith* (Grand Rapids: Eerdmans, 2013), 130–33.

which occurs when the spirit clothes him, Amasai topples any antipathy to David that inhered in Israel's sacred tradition. He exudes the obligatory tenor of deference and acknowledges that David's God is the source of victory. At the end of the day, the warrior-poet is *both* inspired and shrewd. The spirit works wonders in the public realm when Amasai recasts Israel's traditions. The story of Amasai, then, makes this point crystal clear: politics is the natural habitat of the spirit.

After a lengthy hiatus in 1–2 Chronicles, "the spirit was upon Azariah son of Oded" (2 Chron. 15:1, my translation). Like Amasai, Azariah delivers a speech rife with both allusions to Israel's traditions and support for the king (15:2). His words, in fact, are remembered as a prophecy (15:8), a classic combination of inspiration, tradition, and politics.

Next comes the story of Jahaziel, who spoke while "all Judah stood before the LORD, with their little ones, their wives, and their children" (2 Chron. 20:13). The author of 2 Chronicles, in language reminiscent of the judges, notes that "the spirit of the LORD came upon Jahaziel" (20:14). What happens to Jahaziel bears some resemblance to what happened to the judges when the spirit came upon them. Jahaziel's speech dictates a clear *military* strategy. He says,

> Listen, all Judah and inhabitants of Jerusalem, and King Jehoshaphat: Thus says the LORD to you: "Do not fear or be dismayed at this great multitude; for the battle is not yours but God's. Tomorrow go down against them; they will come up by the ascent of Ziz; you will find them at the end of the valley, before the wilderness of Jeruel. This battle is not for you to fight; take your position, stand still, and see the victory of the LORD on your behalf, O Judah and Jerusalem." Do not fear or be dismayed; tomorrow go out against them, and the LORD will be with you. (2 Chron. 20:15–17)

The precision in this speech is salient, including the precise location of the enemy: the ascent of Ziz.

Yet this speech consists of more than military strategy—and here it departs from the inspiration of the judges. The encouragement not to fear, the promise of victory, the realization that the battle is not Judah's to fight but God's—these are *priestly* instructions. According to Deuteronomy, the priest is to speak to the troops prior to battle against superior armies: "Before you engage in battle, the priest shall come forward and speak to the troops, and shall say to them: 'Hear, O Israel! Today you are drawing near to do battle against your enemies. Do not lose heart, or be afraid, or panic, or be in dread of them; for it is the Lord your God who goes with you, to fight for you against your enemies, to give you victory'" (Deut. 20:2–4). When the spirit comes upon Jahaziel, he speaks in the role of the priest in Deuteronomy by gathering the essential ingredients of the priestly instructions to be delivered before battle. Jahaziel is the inspired keeper of the priestly tradition, which he integrates into his own battle plan.

Jahaziel's speech contains distinct allusions to Israelite texts as well. The words "the battle is not yours but God's" recall David's final words to Goliath before he kills the giant: "the battle is the Lord's" (1 Sam. 17:47). The command "Fear not. . . . This battle is not for you to fight; take your position, stand still, and see the victory of the Lord on your behalf" (2 Chron. 20:15, 17) recollects Moses's monumental words to Israel on the cusp of the sea with Egyptian horses and chariots in hot pursuit: "But Moses said to the people, 'Do not be afraid, stand firm, and see the deliverance that the Lord will accomplish for you today'" (Exod. 14:13).

This speech emblematizes the force of the spirit in the public realm. While prophesying in the context of a community of musicians is reminiscent of the community of prophets under whose sway Saul fell, the precision of Jahaziel's speech reveals a keen, if inspired, mind and a mastery of Israel's traditions. His speech, with clear allusions to Israel's literature, combines the directives of a military leader with the encouragement of a priest. Two ends of the spectrum fuse in this speech when the spirit inspires Jahaziel.

Jahaziel is also identified as a member of the Levitic line of the sons of Asaph: "David and the officers of the army also set apart for the service the sons of Asaph, and of Heman, and of Jeduthun, who should prophesy with lyres, harps, and cymbals" (1 Chron. 25:1). Jahaziel was, in short, one of Israel's trained musicians, so his words may have been accompanied by the thrum of music and the beat of drums in preparation for battle—which makes what happens next surprising.[18] Because of his advice, the people of Judah did not need to enter battle at all; they simply looked on and sang praises while their enemies ambushed one another (2 Chron. 20:20–23). Afterward, the victors, who had lifted voices rather than a finger against the enemy, returned to the temple laden with the spoils and weapons of war—harps, lyres, and trumpets—"for the LORD had enabled them to rejoice over their enemies" (20:27–28).

Jahaziel's story echoes Gideon's. The spirit leads—implicitly in the story of Gideon—to a strategy that allows Israel to watch as their enemies destroy themselves. Yet Jahaziel does not himself approach a battle. His job, once inspired, is to offer a keen military strategy that is wrapped in the mantle of the priesthood—and then to sing praise while Israel's enemy implodes. Such a latter-day Gideon is the inspired bearer of a tradition, a singer of Israel's songs, and a military strategist.

The fourth and final inspired figure in 1–2 Chronicles—the Jewish Scriptures as a whole, in fact—is actually a priest, though his words sting with prophetic virulence and lead directly to his death. "The spirit of God clothed Zechariah son of the priest Jehoiada" (my translation), so "he stood above the people and said to them, 'Thus says God: Why do you transgress the commandments of the LORD, so that you cannot prosper? Because you have forsaken the LORD, he has also forsaken you.'" No one would listen. Rather than face the reality of the prophet's opposition, they stoned him, tragically, ironically, in the temple court. While being stoned in the temple court, he cried, "May the LORD see and avenge!" (2 Chron. 24:20–22).

Zechariah, the last inspired speaker in 1–2 Chronicles, illustrates Israel's opposition to its prophets, to its priest-prophets, to men (and only men, apparently) of impeccable priestly, Levitic, or military pedigree. The final word on inspiration in the Hebrew Bible mirrors tragically other Persian era surveys of the history of Israelite prophecy:

> They abandoned the house of the LORD, the God of their ancestors, and served the sacred poles and the idols. And wrath came upon Judah

---

18. What follows musician Jahaziel's speech is not surprising. The king bowed down, face to the ground, with all Judah, worshiping. The Levites and others stood "to praise the LORD, the God of Israel, with a very loud voice" (2 Chron. 20:18–19).

and Jerusalem for this guilt of theirs. Yet [God] sent prophets among them to bring them back to the Lord; they testified against them, but they would not listen. (2 Chron. 24:18–19)

Many years you were patient with them, and warned them by your spirit through your prophets; yet they would not listen. Therefore you handed them over to the peoples of the lands. (Neh. 9:30)

They made their hearts adamant in order not to hear the law and the words that the Lord of hosts had sent by his spirit through the former prophets. Therefore great wrath came from the Lord of hosts. (Zech. 7:12)

The Persian-era version of the rushing, coming, or clothing of the spirit gives testimony to the public power of the spirit embodied by people of learning, masters of the tradition—learned and faithful public intellectuals who studied the past to bequeath a beneficial legacy to their generation. Though the initial impetus of the spirit's onrush lay principally in the stories of Israel's early judges, the impact of the spirit's onrush, according to the Persian-era texts of 1–2 Chronicles, lay elsewhere. Despite a slew of similarities between the book of Judges and 1–2 Chronicles, we have come a long way. In the book of Judges, the spirit inspired acts of liberation; in 1–2 Chronicles, an inspired speaker can urge the people of Judah *not* to fight. In the book of Judges, the spirit inspired action; in 1–2 Chronicles, the spirit inspires only speech—political, prophetic, priestly speech—rife with tradition, striking in its precision. In Judges, the spirit erupted in arenas that were generally free from the corridors of power, where the oppressed yearned for liberation; here, the spirit speaks only in the arena of public politics to kings and those gathered around him. In Judges and 1 Samuel, unexpected leaders received the spirit—the feeble Gideon, the bastard Jephthah, the fickle Samson, the ill-intentioned Saul. Now, those who receive the spirit, though relatively unknown, are people of pedigree—Amasai, chief of the Thirty warriors (1 Chron. 12:18); Azariah, who delivers a "prophecy" directly to the king (2 Chron. 15:1–2); Jahaziel, a trained musician and a descendant of Asaph (2 Chron. 20:14); and Zechariah, a courageous priest (2 Chron. 24:20-22). This swing from the judges and

Israel's enigmatic and troubled first king to the prophet-priests of the Persian era underscores again the symbiosis that existed between tradition and inspiration when it came to political expediency. Old formulas reemerged in new ways, in the midst of new communities, in relation to new speakers, and at the base of new messages.

The stories from Chronicles offer the opportunity to say something significant about the postexilic era—the era after 539 BCE—which is easily caricatured as an epoch of arid spirituality, when legalism is thought to have supplanted the high ethical vision of the prophets and a preoccupation with minutiae is thought to have replaced the great paeans of justice and strains of mercy. This is not the case. The authors of 1–2 Chronicles took a step forward, not backward, when they gathered up Israel's traditions and attributed them to the spirit. The musical tradition. The military tradition. The priestly tradition. Even the prophetic tradition. All of these coalesce in figures such as Amasai, Azariah, Jahaziel, and Zechariah, who do not pay attention to the law at the expense of the spirit. In the stories of these figures, introduced into Israel's story for the first time during the postexilic era, ancient images too easily associated with violence became images of peace, of celebration, of encouragement, of vision. The postexilic period, which fed the era during which Jesus lived, was not arid but alive. It was an era when words like *the spirit clothed* or *the spirit of the* Lord *came upon* came to mean something new, something fresh. It was an era when a respect for tradition *and* a yearning for inspiration fused in the service of the public good—if that public were willing to listen, which, as Zechariah's fate makes clear, some were not.

3

Spirit Resting Upon

Before reading this chapter, explore these texts:

>> Isaiah 11:1–9
>> Isaiah 42:1–9
>> Isaiah 59:20–60:3
>> Isaiah 61

Had an Israelite the wherewithal to write a primer on the art of leadership, he or she would have discovered ample models—*negative* models—in the history of the monarchies of Israel and Judah. Saul, David, and Solomon, each of them, had vulnerable underbellies. Fated nearly from the start, Saul forfeited his reign to David only to spend his remaining years tormented by an evil spirit and a futile quest to destroy his unwanted successor and son's best friend. For his part, David consolidated power in ancient Jebus (Jerusalem), but his heir came from an illicit union with the wife of an officer in his army, whom he effectively murdered. He also spurned his faithful wife and Saul's daughter, Michal, and his later years were marred by a preoccupation with his incestuous family, particularly his vain and arrogant son Absalom, who engineered a coup that David seemed unable to acknowledge. Solomon, the third king of the United

Monarchy and the seed of David's illicit tryst with Bathsheba, had a massive harem, no doubt to establish political alliances, and built the temple for which he is so well known with forced labor. All of this—the harems and the forced-labor pool, as well as the proliferation of horses, a symbol of military prowess—is prohibited in the book of Deuteronomy, perhaps as a reflection of Solomon's excesses.[1]

Solomon taxed his people to the breaking point to build palaces, storehouses, fortifications, the temple, and outposts in the far north and south. His son Rehoboam followed suit by taxing them even more heavily. "My little finger is thicker than my father's loins," Rehoboam boasted immodestly (1 Kings 12:10). As a result of his ill-conceived taxation scheme, the kingdom split in two. Of all the kings of Israel (the Northern Kingdom) and Judah (the Southern Kingdom) to follow, only Hezekiah and Josiah, two Southern kings, are singled out for praise. And with good reason. Northern kings, especially the rulers of the Omride Dynasty in the 700s, ruled over an affluent Israel, but the prophets Hosea and Amos unmasked the injustice of such opulence with scathing judgments against those who drank wine out of bowls, had summer homes in the mountains, and slept on beds of ivory—all the while trampling on the heads of the impoverished and selling debtors for a pair of sandals. The prophetic legacies of Amos and Hosea remain to this day, not because the people welcomed their testimony, but because the doom they portended came about, wealth and power notwithstanding, just a few decades later in 722 BCE, when Assyria, the dominant empire of the ancient Near East at the time, devastated the Northern Kingdom.

The Southern kings of Judah fared no better on the whole. For instance, at a battle at Megiddo in 609 BCE, Pharaoh Neco II killed the stalwart King Josiah and unleashed a string of more fickle and less fearless kings. Josiah's successor, Jehoahaz, lasted three months before being trundled off to Egypt (2 Kings 23:31–35). Pharaoh Neco replaced Jehoahaz with Jehoiakim, who bet on rival empire Babylon, rebelled, and was replaced.[2] His short-lived successor, Je-

---

1. Deut. 17:14–20. This presumes a dating for the composition of Deuteronomy after the reign of Solomon.

2. 2 Kings 24:1 reads, "In his days King Nebuchadnezzar of Babylon came up; Jehoiakim became his servant for three years; then he turned and rebelled against him."

hoiachin, lasted a mere three months before Babylonian emperor Nebuchadnezzar took him into exile and set up Zedekiah as king.[3] Though he reigned for more than ten years, we know only that "Zedekiah rebelled against the king of Babylon" (2 Kings 24:20). That rebellion launched a crisis of great moment. For two years, Babylon besieged Jerusalem, precipitating a dire famine. As the Babylonians breached the city walls, King Zedekiah and his military fled. Caught near Jericho and abandoned by his army, Zedekiah watched as his sons were murdered before he was blinded and bound for Babylon himself (2 King 25:1–7). Shortly afterward, Nebuzaradan, captain of Babylon's bodyguard, wreaked havoc on Jerusalem.[4] The catalog of devastation is breathtaking, ending simply, "So Judah went into exile out of its land" (25:13–21).

The responsibility for the fall of both the Northern and the Southern Kingdoms can be laid largely at the feet of Israel's and Judah's kings, whose ill-advised foreign policies and failure to bring about economic equity raised the hackles of Israel's and Judah's prophets. If an Israelite attempted to write a primer on capable leadership, he or she could not look, therefore, to Israel's kings or queens (among whom can be counted Bathsheba, who schemed on behalf of her son Solomon, and a notorious Jezebel). Such a primer would need to be drawn from elsewhere, perhaps from prophetic imagination, which is precisely the reservoir from which a vision of inspired leadership arose. The spirit would rest, Isaiah imagined, on the right sort of king.

This vision changed over the centuries, though the belief that the spirit rested on such a leader remained remarkably stable. In fact, this image of leadership is confined to the biblical book of Isaiah, which gives it continuity. The composition of the biblical book of Isaiah is believed to have spanned several centuries, from perhaps as early as the late 700s BCE (Isa. 1–39), through a Babylonian era that

3. Nebuchadnezzar's exploits in 597 BCE are narrated vividly in 2 Kings 24:13–15. He did not ravage Jerusalem at that point; he carried off its leading political, military, and skilled leaders. He then appointed Zedekiah in Jehoiachin's stead over an intact Jerusalem. Iain Provan, V. Philips Long, and Tremper Longman (*A Biblical History of Israel* [Louisville: Westminster John Knox, 2015], 381–82), as well as Megan Moore and Brad Kelle (*Biblical History and Israel's Past: The Changing Study of the Bible and History* [Grand Rapids: Eerdmans, 2011], 352–59), offer in-depth analysis of this era.

4. The full story can be found in 2 Kings 25:8–12, 22–26.

brought exile in its train (500s BCE; Isa. 40–55), until the Persian era after return from exile sometime after 539 BCE (Isa. 56–66).[5] It is possible, therefore, to trace a view of inspired leadership as it underwent metamorphoses over the centuries.

Inspired Ruler

Unlike his rural counterpart Micah, Isaiah seems to have walked comfortably in the corridors of power. He was the counselor of kings, a sage charged with giving ballast to a series of leaders, including Jotham, Ahaz, and Hezekiah. His was a momentous time, rife with political intrigue and critical decisions. No sooner had Ahaz, leader of the Southern Kingdom, risen to the throne in his twenties than the Northern Kingdom and Syria had joined in an alliance to resist the Assyrians. Isaiah was adamant that Ahaz should in no way become involved; whether he liked it or not, counseled Isaiah, God would give Ahaz a sign: a young woman would conceive, bear a son, and call his name Immanuel (Isa. 7:14). Ahaz lacked the mettle Isaiah felt he needed; he rejected Isaiah's counsel and appealed for support to the Assyrians, who annexed the Syrians and, just a mere decade later, destroyed the Northern Kingdom. Ahaz seemed to have gotten matters right and Isaiah to have gotten them wrong—his near neighbors, Syria and Israel, were no longer threats—except that Assyria exacted enormous taxes

5. This dating is hardly a matter of consensus, though most scholars consider Isa. 1–39 to be a product of a prophet they call Isaiah of Jerusalem (700s BCE) and chaps. 40–66 to be the product of later prophets who were influenced by these chapters. Many scholars think Isa. 40–66 belongs together, perhaps as a product of the exile in the 500s BCE; these scholars choose not to distinguish between Isa. 40–55 and 56–66. The provenance of Isa. 56–66 is especially disputed, not least because it may be a collection of prophecies rather than a single, unified prophecy. For a brief introduction to the issue, you can consult my *Holy Spirit before Christianity* (Waco: Baylor University Press, 2019), 141, 221nn79–85—though any good commentary on Isaiah will address it.

It also looks as if the entire book underwent a final revision sometime during the Persian era, because the first and final chapters of Isa. 1–66 seem to match. Themes from the earliest chapters reappear in the final chapters: idolatry in gardens, the selfish choices of worshipers, and the metaphors that contrast rotten and good trees. Marvin Sweeney analyzes the process of editing in *Isaiah 1–4 and the Post-exilic Understanding of the Isaianic Tradition* (Berlin: de Gruyter, 1988).

from Ahaz throughout his reign. The cost of doing business with Assyria was high. King Ahaz would never be free of Assyria.

This sort of mistaken policy, which transformed Judah into an Assyrian vassal, prompted Isaiah to imagine a ruler who would not bend to empires or bow to ill-conceived alliances. His conception of a permanent presence of the spirit came to full flower during a politically unstable era, prior to the annihilation of the Northern Kingdom in 722 BCE, when Isaiah dared to speak into a political vacuum. In this era of national quivering, under the unsteady hand of Judah's King Ahaz, Isaiah imagined that

> A shoot shall come out from the stump of Jesse,
>   and a branch shall grow out of his roots.
> The spirit of the Lord shall rest on him,
>   the spirit of wisdom and understanding,
>   the spirit of counsel and might,
>   the spirit of knowledge and the fear of the Lord.
> His delight shall be in the fear of the Lord.
> He shall not judge by what his eyes see,
>   or decide by what his ears hear;
> but with justice he shall judge the poor,
>   and decide with equity for the meek of the earth;
> he shall strike the earth with the rod of his mouth,
>   and with the breath of his lips he shall kill the wicked.
> Righteousness shall be the belt around his waist,
>   and faithfulness the belt around his loins.
>
> The wolf shall live with the lamb,
>   the leopard shall lie down with the kid,
> the calf and the lion and the fatling together,
>   and a little child shall lead them.
> The cow and the bear shall graze,
>   their young shall lie down together;
>   and the lion shall eat straw like the ox.
> The nursing child shall play over the hole of the asp,
>   and the weaned child shall put its hand on the adder's den.
> They will not hurt or destroy
>   on all my holy mountain;
> for the earth will be full of the knowledge of the Lord
>   as the waters cover the sea. (Isa. 11:1–9)

This is not a vision of unmitigated well-being. God has been about the task of lopping off geopolitical boughs, cutting down the tallest trees, bringing lofty branches low, hacking down forests with an axe (10:33–34). Out of this destructive swath emerges not a cedar of Lebanon but a stump. There are no psalms of installation, no songs of coronation. There is a stump, the root of a nondescript man.

The expression of tenacity in this oracle is subtle but unmistakable. I know this because I am married to a gardener. Nearly fifteen years ago, she and I planted an Akebia vine on our Seattle deck. Year by year it grew. Then, one year, Priscilla pruned our cherished Akebia vine until all that was left were gnarly, brittle branches. I was sure she had murdered it. But that Akebia came back lush and green. A shoot came out of the stump of the Akebia; a branch grew out of its roots.

Isaiah's nation, Judah, was like an ancient Akebia in Priscilla's ruthless hands, pruned to near nonexistence in the late 700s. King Ahaz had won freedom from Israel and Syria by bringing the colossal hand of Assyria down on the countryside around Jerusalem. Isaiah was displeased, so he offered an alternative vision of leadership.

The ruler who emerges from the ruins of Assyria's relentless march will not bring back the glory days of King David, Jesse's son. He will not add palaces and fortresses and stables for hundreds of horses, the way Solomon did. This is a stump, after all. Yet what a ruler he will be! His rule derives exclusively from the spirit of the Lord that rests upon him and grants him intellectual and practical skills needed for peacetime leadership (understanding and wisdom), skills of developing various strategies and perhaps leading in battle (counsel and courage),[6] and devotion to God through worship (knowledge and fear of God).[7] The spirit's resting presence, which occurs four times in a short space, underscores that these qualities are given from the Lord.

The weapon this ruler wields is a word: the rod of his mouth and the breath—*rûaḥ*—of his lips. We know now that this is not mere breath or material life. This *rûaḥ*, like Job's, is the source of wisdom. This *rûaḥ* is resplendent with integrity and truth. This *rûaḥ* destroys the wicked, not with swords and spears but with justice, equity, and

---

6. In Prov. 8:14, this pair is also used to describe peacetime leadership.
7. A related description of this anointed figure can be found in Isa. 9:6–7.

faithfulness. There is not a whiff of political vacillation in Isaiah's vision; there is ballast, spirit resting upon the ruler and spirit rising from within, extinguishing enemies with a word.[8]

These are precisely the qualities that human beings can only make a pretense of exhibiting. Assyria's arrogance impels it to make an ill-advised claim to wisdom and understanding (Isa. 10:13). Judah's counsel (8:10) comes to nothing, and its mighty warriors fall in battle (3:25). As a consequence, Judah is void of knowledge (5:13) and rife with misguided fear (7:4; 8:12–13; 10:24). Not so the leader upon whom the spirit rests. What nations, including Isaiah's own, lack, this inspired ruler embodies: understanding and wisdom, counsel and courage, knowledge and a fear of God.

At the heart of this ruler's vocation lies judging on behalf of the poor. Clothed with justice as his belt and faithfulness as his undergarment, he will bring about justice, not with violence but with the rod of his mouth; his inspired words alone will destroy the wicked.

As the oracle now stands, Isaiah imaginatively expands the reign of the righteous ruler to encompass the entire natural world. Wolf lies down with lamb, leopard with kid, calf and lion and fatling together—with a little child at their head. Cow and bear will graze. The lion will eat straw. A nursing child will play over a snake's hole and a weaned child over a serpent's den. Utter justice, in brief, will issue in utter peace.

Still, it would be a mistake to see this as a utopian vision. The force of this vision, its dynamic, lies in how hard-fought justice is. The ruler's inspired leadership does not play out naturally in a peaceable world full of generous people living kindly, loving mercy, and walking humbly with their God.[9] The new Eden, where lions lie down with

---

8. This quadrilateral of qualities—the spirit, justice, the spoken word, and the power to annihilate enemies—is similar to Micah's conception of his prophetic role. Micah, too, claims to speak powerfully because of the spirit, justice, and power. The sole difference is that Micah already has the spirit within him as a permanent endowment, while the notion of the resting of the spirit upon the ideal ruler flows from the image of the king as one who is anointed with oil (e.g., 1 Sam. 10:1; 16:13; Ps. 2:2). In both instances, Micah's and this ruler's, the spirit is conceived of as a permanent endowment. The spirit in Mic. 3:8 is presumably from birth; it is the ruler's from the moment the spirit begins to rest upon him or her.

9. Mic. 6:8.

lambs, will also have within it a nursing child surrounded by snakes, a weaned child playing in a snake pit. This vision of harmony and wholeness is offered to a fractured people in need of security that will be gathered "from Assyria, from Egypt, from Pathros, from Ethiopia, from Elam, from Shinar, from Hamath, and from the coastlands of the sea" (Isa. 11:11). Isaiah's rural contemporary, Micah, dreamed of this sort of community and commitment (Mic. 6:8). Isaiah is warier—an urban dweller too close to kings to avert his eyes from the pitfall of political indecision. The spirit that will rest upon the ruler from the root of Jesse, inspiring with understanding and wisdom, counsel and courage, knowledge and fear of God, will *not* generate utopia. That spirit will generate something more this-worldly: justice for the poor and equity for the meek in a world fraught with political peril.

Inspired Servant

Nearly two centuries passed before a prophet in the line of Isaiah picked up the themes of Isaiah 11:1–9. During those centuries, a great deal happened, not least the devastation of Jerusalem, the brutal end of the monarchy, and the forced deportation of Judah's elite—men and women like the prophet Ezekiel—to Babylon in 597 and 587 BCE. With the Persian Empire on the horizon—they would soon eclipse Babylon—there was no hope that a king would once again sit on the throne in Judah. The spirit, therefore, rests now not on a monarch but upon someone whom the prophet calls the *servant*:

> Here is my [God's] servant, whom I uphold,
>   my chosen, in whom my soul delights;
> I have put my spirit upon him;
>   he will bring forth justice to the nations.
> He will not cry or lift up his voice,
>   or make it heard in the street;
> a bruised reed he will not break,
>   and a dimly burning wick he will not quench;
>   he will faithfully bring forth justice.

He will not grow faint or be crushed
  until he has established justice in the earth;
  and the coastlands wait for his teaching.

Thus says God, the LORD,
  who created the heavens and stretched them out,
  who spread out the earth and what comes from it,
who gives breath to the people upon it
  and spirit to those who walk in it:
I am the LORD, I have called you in righteousness,
  I have taken you by the hand and kept you;
I have given you as a covenant to the people,
  a light to the nations,
  to open the eyes that are blind,
to bring out the prisoners from the dungeon,
  from the prison those who sit in darkness.
I am the LORD, that is my name;
  my glory I give to no other,
  nor my praise to idols.
See, the former things have come to pass,
  and new things I now declare;
before they spring forth,
  I tell you of them. (Isa. 42:1–9)

It is difficult to identify this servant (42:1), who could represent an array of individuals or communities: the nation Israel (41:8–10); a faithful remnant within Israel; a prophetic individual; Moses, who is explicitly identified as God's servant and is associated with judgment and teaching;[10] or even, though unlikely, the Persian ruler Cyrus, who is designated the LORD's anointed because he restores the exiles to the land (45:1).[11] Any of these alternatives is plausible, with telling implications: there is a wide chasm between the identification of the servant as Moses or Cyrus.[12]

10. E.g., Exod. 14:31; Num. 12:8; Josh. 1:2; Neh. 1:7; Ps. 105:26.
11. Raymond Collins's entry, "Servant of the LORD, the," in *New Interpreter's Dictionary of the Bible*, ed. Katharine Doob Sakenfeld (Nashville: Abingdon, 2006), 5:192–95, provides a reliable introduction to the so-called Servant Songs in Isa. 40–55.
12. Another difficulty in this brief description is the meaning of justice, *mišpāṭ*, which is the center of gravity of this text. Although it is translated above by the word *justice*, its meaning is far more contested, so that it is simply not clear what

Even if we cannot identify this servant with a figure of history, we can garner insight from this rich reflection. The servant's message is characterized as *tôrâ*, "teaching," for which the coastlands wait. The source of such teaching becomes evident in a later depiction of the servant: "The Lord GOD has given me the tongue of a teacher, that I may know how to sustain the weary with a word. Morning by morning he wakens—wakens my ear to listen as those who are taught. The Lord GOD has opened my ear, and I was not rebellious, I did not turn backward" (Isa. 50:4–5).

The pairing of teaching and learning in this autobiographical snippet is an essential ingredient of inspired prophecy. The Hebrew root *lmd*, "to teach" and "to learn," frequently describes teaching and training on various topics, such as God's statutes and ordinances (Deut. 4:1, 5), about which parents are commanded, "Teach them to your children, talking about them when you are at home and when you are away, when you lie down and when you rise" (11:19).[13] Teaching—learning too—is a matter of repetition, recurrence, recitation. Learning—teaching too—takes place morning by morning rather than through the spontaneous combustion of charisma. This is an indispensable insight because it challenges any effort to separate the spirit from dogged, daily learning. The border between discipline and inspiration, from the perspective of this inspired servant, is diaphanous.

For the nations, the teaching of Torah arrives as light. The servant is "a light to the nations, to open the eyes that are blind, to bring out the prisoners from the dungeon, from the prison those who

---

the servant will bring. The servant may offer up justice, *mišpāṭ*, in the sense of a positive judicial decision as a declaration of innocence (e.g., Isa. 40:27; 49:4; 50:8; Ps. 37:6); he or she may offer justice, *mišpāṭ*, in a negative judicial decision that brings judgment to the nations because their gods are nothing (Isa. 41:1–5, 21–29). Justice may also mean the establishment of justice, of God's design for the nations, with Israel at their center (40:14; 51:4). Or it may refer principally to a way of behaving, as in Jer. 5:4–5 and 8:7, where justice, *mišpāṭ*, and teaching, *tôrâ*, occur in tandem to describe Israel's failure to act correctly.

13. This meaning occurs predominantly in the Hebrew *piel* stem, which is used of teaching songs (2 Sam. 1:18), training soldiers for war (2 Sam. 22:35; Ps. 18:34 [MT 18:35]), and in the related *pual* stem, skilled singers (1 Chron. 25:7). Such teaching is also aligned with "study" in Ezra 7:10: "For Ezra had set his heart to study the law of the LORD, and to do it, and to teach the statutes and ordinances in Israel."

sit in darkness" (Isa. 42:6–7). The capacity of the servant to dispel darkness among the nations is one of the most striking dimensions of this figure, whose experience of Babylonian exile, we might expect, would lead to disdain rather than hope for the nations. On the contrary, God's claim that the servant will be "a light to the nations" (42:6) aligns perfectly with God's priorities: "Listen to me, my people, and give heed to me, my nation; for a teaching will go out from me, and my justice for a light to the peoples. I will bring near my deliverance swiftly, my salvation has gone out and my arms will rule the peoples; the coastlands wait for me, and for my arm they hope" (51:4–5).

To the prophet's own nation in exile, the message is one of comfort; the servant has the tongue of a disciple to "know how to sustain the weary with a word" (Isa. 50:4). The whole of Isaiah 40–55 begins as a tender word of comfort (40:1) for a wearied nation:

> Have you not known? Have you not heard?
> The LORD is the everlasting God,
>   the Creator of the ends of the earth.
> He does not faint or *grow weary*;
>   his understanding is unsearchable.
> He gives power to the *faint*,
>   and strengthens the powerless.
> Even youths will faint and *be weary*,
>   and the young will fall exhausted;
> but those who wait for the LORD shall renew their strength,
>   they shall mount up with wings like eagles,
> they shall run and not be weary,
>   they shall walk and not *faint*. (Isa. 40:28–31, italics
>   added).

The giving of the spirit upon the servant inspires teaching for a wearied Israel.

The servant's teaching, though encouraging to his own people and perfectly aligned with God's vision for the nations, leads to a life of suffering and pain. The seeds of suffering are muted in the first description of the servant. The verb *ṣāʿaq*, translated as "cry" in the line, "He will not cry or lift up his voice" (Isa. 42:2), could simply mean "cry loudly," though the word refers throughout the book of Isaiah to cries *of anguish* (19:20; 33:7; 46:7; 65:14). The servant will not cry in anguish publicly. The servant will not grow weary or be crushed until after his task of bringing justice to the earth is successfully completed and his teaching reaches the coastlands.

Later still, the prophet ignites fiery opposition.[14] "I gave my back to those who struck me, and my cheeks to those who pulled out the beard; I did not hide my face from insult and spitting" (Isa. 50:6). He sets his face like flint to the task ahead and, in an intriguing wordplay on the Hebrew root *klm*, contends that he can endure insults (*mikkəlimmôt*) unashamed (*niklāmətî*).[15] He eventually becomes a man of sorrows, acquainted with sickness, one from whom others hide, despised, of no account, struck down, afflicted, wounded, crushed, punished, oppressed, silent like a lamb before the slaughter, cut off from the living, tormented for the transgression of God's people, buried with the wicked, crushed with pain, anguished, poured out to death, counted among transgressors—all of this even though he has never taken up violence or uttered a word of deceit (52:13–53:12).

Perhaps the opposition he garners is the result of a new theme that emerges in the figure of the servant: the spirit inspires a view of the world that is expansive, inclusive, with *tôrâ* taken to the coastlands and light taken to the nations. This vision is not shared by most of the prophet's contemporaries, whose own love of country flies in the face of God's love of *other* countries. This is not a natural vision. This is certainly not a comfortable vision. But it is an *inspired* vision. And it is a vision that leads to conflict, that pits patriots against the prophet. Because this vision of the world, with priority given to the nations and not *a* nation, flies in the face of nationalism, it breeds conflict, especially from the children of those who had endured forced resettlement in Babylon.

From this vantage point, the Old Testament delivers another crucial insight about the spirit: it would be a grave mistake to identify the presence of the spirit with a lack of conflict. It would be a misjudgment to regard acquiescence to the world as it is, with its

14. There is a close connection between these autobiographical statements by the prophet and the role of the servant in Isa. 40–55.
15. Isa. 50:6–7.

arbitrary borders, as the sort of peace the spirit generates. Nothing can be further from the truth, at least in light of this portrait of the servant, whose commitment to the world, not as it is but as it should be, makes him or her restive and ready to teach, not just in Jerusalem but along the coasts.

The inspiration of the messianic ruler (Isa. 11:1–9) has undergone a metamorphosis in Isaiah 40–55; the impact of the more than 150 years separating them, with the advent of exile, has been inevitable. While the messianic ruler, according to Isaiah 11, would usher in a precarious justice, the servant's job is harder still. From a position without apparent privilege, he proclaims a destiny of light for ancient Near Eastern empires, one of which decades earlier had devastated his own nation, Judah. This is an unpalatable vision for an exilic community that has paid its penalty, served its term, paid double for all its sins (40:2). Perhaps the disparity between their experience and the servant's vocation is too much to bear. Perhaps the servant is sacrificed on the altar of his own capacious vision for the nations.

Inspired Prophet

We may be tempted now to fly straight to the famed text in Isaiah 61 that fired the imagination of Jesus: "The spirit of the Lord GOD is upon me . . . to bring good news to the oppressed." In the meantime, one snippet of Hebrew prose tucked into a pocket of poetry does not quite fit the trajectory from Isaiah 11 through Isaiah 42 to Isaiah 61—but offers insight into the spirit nonetheless.

We will start with what comes before this text, which is full of hope for the nations: "So those in the west shall fear the name of the LORD, and those in the east, his glory; for he will come like a pent-up stream that the wind of the LORD drives on" (Isa. 59:19). That word *wind* is indeed *rûaḥ*, so that wind is not *mere* wind but wind *of the Lord*. This is familiar territory, like the story of Moses and the elders in the desert, when a wind from the Lord drove quail to the outskirts of the camp. God is at it again, driving dammed streams to overflow, only this time the wind drives not quail but fear of God and God's glory. This time, too, God's spirit-wind comes not only to the east, to the small refugee camp in the desert, but to the east *and* the west—to the whole world. This is no gentle breeze. This is a gale that causes a stream to surge.

What follows is equally familiar:

> Arise, shine; for your light has come,
>   and the glory of the LORD has risen upon you.
> For darkness shall cover the earth,
>   and thick darkness the peoples;
> but the LORD will arise upon you,
>   and his glory will appear over you.
> Nations shall come to your light,
>   and kings to the brightness of your dawn. (Isa. 60:1–3)

The prophet has taken up the language of Isaiah 42, in which the servant, a light to the nations, brings forth justice.

Compared to the wideness of God's mercy that precedes and follows, Isaiah 59:21 seems narrow, unoriginal, and pedestrian: "And as for me, this is my covenant with them, says the LORD: my spirit that is upon you, and my words that I have put in your mouth, shall not depart out of your mouth, or out of the mouths of your children, or out of the mouths of your children's children, says the LORD, from now on and forever." This promise looks at first blush prosaic and predictable—an uninventive extension of the earlier promises of Ezekiel and Jeremiah, who had made similar promises decades earlier:

> A new heart I will give you, and a new spirit I will put within you; and I will remove from your body the heart of stone and give you a heart of flesh. I will put my spirit within you, and make you follow my statutes and be careful to observe my ordinances. Then you shall live in the land that I gave to your ancestors; and you shall be my people, and I will be your God. (Ezek. 36:26–28)

> The days are surely coming, says the LORD, when I will make a new covenant with the house of Israel and the house of Judah. It will not be like the covenant that I made with their ancestors when I took them by the hand to bring them out of the land of Egypt—a covenant that they broke, though I was their husband, says the LORD. But this is the covenant that I will make with the house of Israel after those days,

says the LORD: I will put my law within them, and I will write it on their hearts; and I will be their God, and they shall be my people. No longer shall they teach one another, or say to each other, "Know the LORD," for they shall all know me, from the least of them to the greatest, says the LORD; for I will forgive their iniquity, and remember their sin no more. (Jer. 31:31–34)

These are sweeping promises, but they envisage only the restoration of Judah after the Babylonian exile—not justice for the nations. It looks as if the prophet in Isaiah 59 has retreated to follow the same hopeful vein for Israel alone.

Not so. The promise in Isaiah 59:21 is not about the nation; it is about an individual. In fact, it is directed to the prophet in whose mouth alone God's words are to be found.[16] God does indeed make a covenant with Israel—but exclusively through this solitary individual, upon whom the spirit rests, and his descendants. These words are reminiscent of God's words to the prophet in Isaiah 51:16: "I have put my words in your mouth, and hidden you in the shadow of my hand, stretching out the heavens and laying the foundations of the earth, and saying to Zion, 'You are my people.'"[17]

This is a powerful affirmation of the prophet's legacy. It is a *necessary* affirmation of the prophet's legacy as well. If the prophet is in any way connected to the servant, then we know his or her destiny: to be rejected by countrymen and -women and to be despised,

16. Each occurrence of "you" or "your" is in the second person singular. This seems to be a promise not about Israel as a whole but about one person and his descendants. Though it is possible that God addresses the whole nation as one person, it is more likely, for a few reasons, that this is an individual. First, in other passages, such as Isa. 44:3, in which the singular refers to the nation, Israel is understood eponymously—that is, as an individual who is identified variously as Jacob, Israel, and Jeshurun (44:1–2); naturally, then, the pronouns will be in the singular. This is not the case in Isa. 59:21. Second, throughout the entire Isaiah corpus, the spirit *rests* exclusively upon individuals (11:2; 42:1; 61:1), though it can be *poured out* on an entire nation. Third, the placement of God's words in "your [singular] mouth" is the classic expression for the inspiration of an *individual* prophet. When a group is in mind, as in 1 Kings 22:23, God gives a lying spirit "in the mouth of all these your prophets."

17. A widow whose son has been raised confesses to Elijah, "Now I know that you are a man of God, and that the word of the LORD in your mouth is truth" (1 Kings 17:24). Jeremiah recalls that "the LORD said to me, 'Now I have put my words in your mouth'" (Jer. 1:9).

disfigured, denigrated as a result of the good news of justice brought to the empires that had destroyed his or her grandparents' homeland.[18] Given the destiny that lay ahead, the prophet could choose either to lay aside this expansive vision, to view it as an expendable element of an otherwise robust prophetic call, or to claim it and proclaim it, enduring the suffering that lay ahead for the sake of the legacy that lay still further—and just as certainly—in the future, "from now on and forever." The prophet claims and proclaims this calling.

Two centuries earlier, during the mid-700s BCE, Hosea declared that the Israelites had said, "The prophet is a fool, the man of the spirit is mad!" (Hosea 9:7). The Israelites did not say this because Hosea's behavior was manic. They said it because his prophecies of doom were inconceivable. Israel was at the height of affluence, with political alliances in place to stave off the growing threat of Assyrian domination. Hosea relentlessly railed against those alliances and saw through their ostensible protective shell. Israel thought he was mad because they simply could not see through their prosperity and political pacts to the vulnerability that would, Hosea knew, bring them to their knees within a few short decades.

This sort of inspired doggedness is what fuels prophetic conviction. Sustaining a vision, even an inspired vision, that runs counter to the status quo is no small feat. It demands quiet commitment for the long haul (Isa. 42:2). It entails daily discipline and receptiveness to God's alternative vision for the world (50:5–6). It requires the ability to look beyond the cusp of the near future to an enduring legacy (59:21). To have God say, "My spirit is upon you," is to embody the all-encompassing vocation demanded not only by a life of justice but by a life committed to the seemingly futile effort of urging others to devote themselves to justice as well. The ability to endure a life of apparent futility—Isaiah, we may remember, was first called to make the people's ears dull and unreceptive (6:10)—is an essential dimension of inspiration. This resolve, this determination, is life in the spirit from a prophetic perspective.

---

18. Such a scenario, in which men and women oppressed their countrymen and -women, is evident during the postexilic era in a telling description in Neh. 5:1–5. Desperate Israelites appear to have forced other Israelites to pledge their fields, houses, and vineyards and to offer their sons and daughters as slaves simply to survive.

Inspired Liberator

In a splash a lavishness defying the notion that the poor deserve only the crumbs off the table, a prophet continues to express the vitality of justice:

> The spirit of the Lord God is upon me,
>> because the Lord has anointed me;
> he has sent me to bring good news to the oppressed,
>> to bind up the brokenhearted,
> to proclaim liberty to the captives,
>> and release to the prisoners;
> to proclaim the year of the Lord's favor,
>> and the day of vengeance of our God;
>> to comfort all who mourn;
> to provide for those who mourn in Zion—
>> to give them a garland instead of ashes,
> the oil of gladness instead of mourning,
>> the mantle of praise instead of a faint spirit.
> They will be called oaks of righteousness,
>> the planting of the Lord, to display his glory.
> They shall build up the ancient ruins,
>> they shall raise up the former devastations;
> they shall repair the ruined cities,
>> the devastations of many generations. (Isa. 61:1–4)

A garland, the oil of gladness, a mantle of praise—these are not the begrudging upshot of mandatory alms. Nor are "oaks of righteousness" and "planting of the Lord" metaphors of survival; they are the stuff of massive forests and vibrant gardens. This final oracle of the spirit's resting is not about the alleviation of poverty; it is about healing and liberation and victory laps and celebrations and centuries-old forests and trees of life. It is a celebration of the Year of Jubilee, the fiftieth year, when every debt was wiped clean (Lev. 25:8–17). This is a wonderfully outlandish vision, not just of Judah restored but of Judah restored in such a way that everyone, top to bottom, rich to poor, shares in God's glory. It is a manifesto that everyone—the descendants of the elite taken into exile and the descendants of tenant farmers who had not been taken into exile—would together rebuild Jerusalem and reap the benefits of divine blessing.

This is no empty speech, in light of the powerful images of inclusion that saturate Isaiah 56–66, with its vivid image of topsy-turvy worship—eunuchs keeping Sabbath (Isa. 56:3–5), foreigners at the heart of the temple (56:3, 6–7), and outcasts gathered (56:8). This prophet is able to create with a word a new heaven (65:17), though not without a new earth that quakes with a shift in social templates: eunuchs embrace the promise to Abraham and Sarah, foreigners lead worship, and the poor wear victory garlands.

This prophet paints with words from another palette altogether, sculpting with speech a statuesque people whose feet are firmly planted in justice. The prophet does not do this from scratch. This mission is rooted in the wisdom of the inspired messiah (Isa. 11:1–4) and the vision of justice for the nations lying at the core of the exilic servant's teaching (42:1–7). Like inspired leaders of earlier eras, the only weapon wielded is the spoken word; this is the rod of the ideal ruler (Isa. 11), the sword of the servant (Isa. 50), the word God puts in the prophet's mouth (Isa. 59), and the speech of the liberator (Isa. 61).

This vision of justice also changed over the years as Israel's political situation shifted. It moved from a messianic ruler (Isa. 11) to a suffering servant (Isa. 42) to a prophetic recipient of the covenant (Isa. 59) to a champion of the oppressed (Isa. 61). As political angst (Isa. 11) turned to the Babylonian exile (Isa. 42) and the challenges of rebuilding during the Persian era (Isa. 59; 61), the universal tendency that is hinted at in Isaiah 11 swelled to encompass proselytes from distant coastlands (Isa. 42) and then narrowed, though not in any sort of parochial way, to an intense preoccupation with the plight of the poor in Israel (Isa. 61).

Peculiar in this oracle, at least to readers reared in an era of political jockeying for power through self-promotion, is how little we know about the leader on whom the spirit rests and how much more we know about the people he or she liberates. The inspired one in Isaiah 61 is only *me*, but those whom the inspired one restores are the oppressed, the brokenhearted, the captives, the prisoners, and those who mourn. In fact, we glimpse especially what the inspired leader will do: bring good news; bind up; proclaim liberty, release, the year of God's favor, and the day of vengeance; comfort; provide; and give a garland, the oil of gladness, and a mantle of praise. The initiative is staggering, the generosity astounding. This is, of course, as it should be for those inspired by the spirit. Self-aggrandizement yields to emancipation, avarice to assistance, ambition to liberation in the shadow of the spirit.

4

Spirit Passed On

Before reading this chapter, explore these texts:

>> Numbers 11:16–30
>> Numbers 27:12–23
>> Deuteronomy 34:7–12
>> 1 Kings 22:1–40
>> 2 Kings 2:1–18

In a bizarre story wedged into the first book of Kings, we meet Micaiah ben Imlah, a little-known prophet willing to put his life on the line for what he believes to be true. As the story begins, the Northern Kingdom and Syria (just to its north) have been at peace for three years. Three years too many, apparently, for King Jehoshaphat of the Southern Kingdom, who comes to King Ahab of the Northern Kingdom and offers to enter into a political alliance in order to defeat Syria. In cahoots now, the kings are ready to go, except that King Jehoshaphat recommends they seek a word of the Lord. They do, and four hundred prophets under the leadership of a certain Zedekiah champion King Ahab's plan. Jehoshaphat, skeptical about how quickly the prophets agreed with their king, asks if there is another prophet anywhere. King Ahab says there is—Micaiah ben Imlah—but he hates him and has locked him up because Micaiah always has a negative word for him. Jehoshaphat asks to hear from Micaiah, who surprisingly—and here the irony begins in earnest—tells the king what he wants to hear. Ahab knows something is off—Micaiah does not usually agree with the other four hundred prophets—so, oddly enough, the king demands the truth. "How many times must I make you swear to tell me nothing but the truth in the name of the LORD?" pleads the king (1 Kings 22:16). So Micaiah tells the truth: the king will die in a lost cause. Ahab then turns to his new ally from the south and says, ironically again, since he forced Micaiah's hand, "Did I not tell you that he would not prophesy anything favorable about me, but only disaster?" (22:18).

Whether to satisfy Ahab or to twist the knife in further—or both—Micaiah tells him about a vision he had. In the heavenly court, God asks for volunteers. "Who will entice Ahab, so that he may go up and fall at Ramoth-gilead?" asks God (1 Kings 22:20).[1] One of the spirits in the heavenly court volunteers: "I will go out and be a lying spirit in the mouth of all his prophets" (22:22). Though vivid, even shocking, there is nothing particularly novel in this vision. Prophets typically had prophetic opponents. Micah, for example, despised other prophets, who, like Zedekiah and his cronies in the story of Micaiah, declared what the king wanted to hear (Mic. 3:1–8). Ezekiel spared no expense in denigrating his opponents: "Therefore this is what the Sovereign LORD says: Because of your false words and lying visions, I am against you, declares the Sovereign LORD. My hand will be against the prophets who see false visions and utter lying divinations" (Ezek. 13:8–9 NIV). The lying spirit—the deceptive *rûaḥ*—is a striking image but not a new one.[2]

A good deal could be said at this point about the nature of inspiration, not least how difficult it can be to distinguish between true

1. This scenario suggests the presence of an angelic retinue which gathers around God, as in Isa. 6 and Ps. 103:19–22.
2. The intervening references to the spirit (1 Kings 22:22–23) are to "a lying spirit in the mouth of all his [Ahab's] prophets." The unusual expression, "a spirit in the mouth," is due perhaps to the influence of Deut. 18:18, which refers to a prophet and to the promise, "I will put my words in the mouth of the prophet, who shall speak to them everything that I command."

and false prophecy. One criterion of discernment is the relationship of the spirit to the status quo. Like the servant of Isaiah 42, Micaiah speaks *against* the status quo. Consensus is *not* truth; the assurance of four hundred prophets who owe their livelihoods to the king is worth less than one message cutting across the consensus.

Another criterion has to do with concreteness. What Micaiah says is not vague or vacuously spiritual. His prediction of Ahab's death is clear: "I saw all of Israel scattered on the mountains, like sheep that have no shepherd" (1 Kings 22:17). In fact, as a true prophet, he hangs his fate on his message: "If you return in peace," he says to King Ahab, "the LORD has not spoken by me" (22:28). A word of the spirit, from the standpoint of this story, must be specific.[3]

The story continues with its climax in a confrontation between Zedekiah, head of the four hundred, and Micaiah. Zedekiah challenges Micaiah's authority, which is where our study of the spirit *passed on* begins: "Which way did the spirit of the LORD pass from me to speak to you?" (1 Kings 22:24). This could be taken to mean simply, "Why are you right—and I am wrong?" But more is probably meant. The crucial word in this indictment for understanding the nature of the spirit is the verb, "to cross over," "to pass," for it recalls the transference of the spirit of God from Saul to David. The parallel between 1 Kings 22:24 and 1 Samuel 16:13–23 suggests that the spirit—and authority with it—can pass as a whole from one living person to another. In both instances, the former loses the power of the spirit, which the latter gains.

This is not an easy concept to grasp. It certainly was not for the ancient Greek translators of the Hebrew Scriptures, who translated the Hebrew of 1 Kings 22:24, "Which way did the spirit of the Lord pass from me to speak to you?" into Greek as "What kind of a spirit of the Lord has spoken in you?"[4] The question in the Greek translation is not about *how* the spirit passed from Zedekiah to Micaiah but *what sort of* spirit has spoken in Zedekiah's prophetic opponent, Micaiah.

3. Michael Welker, in *God the Spirit* (Minneapolis: Fortress, 1994), 50–74, offers an important analysis of this story, including a discussion of criteria by which it is possible to distinguish false prophecy from true.

4. Unless otherwise indicated, English translations of the Greek Old Testament are from NETS.

While the passing of the spirit from one person to another may be a difficult concept to grasp, it is a *biblical* concept nonetheless.

Moses and the Elders—and Saul

The transferal of the spirit from one person to another is no less puzzling in a story told of Moses and seventy-two elders in the wilderness. This story raises the question of the role that physical proximity plays in the spread of the spirit; in these stories, at least, physical nearness is requisite to the passing of the spirit.

In this story, Moses complained that the people were too much of a burden for him to carry; God responded by commanding Moses to gather seventy of the registered elders at the tent of meeting where, God promised, "I will come down and talk with you there; and I will take some of the spirit that is on you and put it on them; and they shall bear the burden of the people along with you so that you will not bear it all by yourself" (Num. 11:17). Moses then "gathered seventy elders of the people, and placed them all around the tent. Then the LORD came down in the cloud and spoke to him, and took some of the spirit that was on him and put it on the seventy elders; and when the spirit rested upon them, they prophesied. But they did not do so again" (11:24–25).[5] This is a baffling story, which needs to be taken apart bit by bit and put back together, if we are to learn about the spirit from it.

It is baffling, in part, because of how little is said about the nature of prophesying. Usually, the elders' prophesying is understood to mean a fall into prophetic frenzy, "a circumstance of rapturous excitement, ecstatic inspiration and frenzy, into which one falls fortuitously and perhaps by coercion . . . or in which one is 'beside oneself' for a limited time."[6] This interpretation is not apparent in the story itself; it arises instead from the recurrence of the same Hebrew verb in the story of Saul, who is said to have fallen into prophetic

---

5. I offer a detailed analysis of this story in "Prophecy in Ancient Israel: The Case of the Ecstatic Elders," *Catholic Biblical Quarterly* 65 (2003): 503–21.

6. Joachim Jeremias, "נָבִיא," in *Theological Lexicon of the Old Testament*, ed. E. Jenni and C. Westermann (Peabody, MA: Hendrickson, 1997), 2:704.

ecstasy (1 Sam. 19:23–24; see 10:9–13). In this light, "the effect of the spirit resting on the elders was that they fell into a prophetic frenzy, just as the messengers of Saul, and ultimately Saul himself, were overpowered by the spirit and made, even against their will, to prophesy . . ."[7]

The assumption here is that Saul's experience of prophesying unlocks what is left unsaid about the elders' prophesying in the desert. The same Hebrew root, *nb'*, in the same *hithpael* stem, occurs in both stories, suggesting parallel experiences. The communal dimension is there in both stories, too, in the group of prophets and the group of prophesying elders, suggesting perhaps the contagion of ecstasy. And there is a measure of approval in both stories; Saul was transformed into another person (1 Sam. 10:6), suggesting that the elders, too, are transformed into another sort of people. Moses welcomes this experience—even when it happens to two elders who have not joined the seventy. Moses seems almost giddy when he says, "Would that all the LORD's people were prophets, and that the Lord would put his spirit on them!" (Num. 11:29). In light of the story of Saul, it is difficult to interpret prophesying as anything but a fall into frenzy.

There is a problem, however, with this interpretation. How Moses's administrative burden is lessened by putting seventy elders into a state of ecstasy is difficult to imagine.[8] In fact, if we look more closely, we will see that they did not, according to this story, fall into ecstasy. Something else, something more momentous, something more closely aligned with the grand experience at Mount Sinai, occurred.

7. George B. Gray, *Numbers*, International Critical Commentary (Edinburgh: T&T Clark, 1903), 113. George Montague, in *Holy Spirit: Growth of a Biblical Tradition* (Peabody, MA: Hendrickson, 1994), 15, observes, "There is no indication of the content of their [the elders'] prophesying, and the sense is therefore probably that of prophetic ecstasy, as in 1 Sam 10:5ff. and 19:20ff." Baruch Levine, *Numbers 1–20: A New Translation with Introduction and Commentary*, Anchor Bible 4A (Garden City, NY: Doubleday, 1993), 340, adds to the consensus: "The verb *hitnabbe'* 'to experience prophetic ecstasy' describes what happens physically and emotionally when the irresistible spirit of God seizes a person. This particular form of the verb *naba'* 'to pronounce, utter prophecy' is best known from the biblical stories about Saul (1 Sam 10:5–6; 18:29; 19:23–24)."

8. Martin Noth, *Numbers: A Commentary*, Old Testament Library (Philadelphia: Westminster, 1968), 89.

The Elders in the Wilderness and the Elders at Sinai

The story of the prophesying elders is a mirror image of the elders who ascended Mount Sinai with Moses. In short, Numbers 11 corresponds to Exodus 16–24. Numbers 11, for example, repeats elements that already took place in Exodus 16: the complaint about food (Exod. 16:2–3; Num. 11:1, 4–6), the daily gift of manna (Exod. 16:16–21; Num. 11:6–9), and the arrival of quail (Exod. 16:13; Num. 11:31–34).

Even more striking are the affinities that exist between Exodus 18 and Numbers 11, both of which address the challenge of Moses's burden. In Exodus 18:18, Moses's father-in-law Jethro watches Moses keenly, then notes, "the task is too heavy for you;" Moses in Numbers 11:14 says of his people, "they are too heavy for me." In Exodus 18:21–22, Jethro advises Moses to appoint officers who will bear the burden with him; God responds with identical words in Numbers 11:16–17, telling Moses that the elders will bear the burden with him. The elders' role in both stories, Exodus 18 and Numbers 11, is precisely the same: to aid Moses with the burdens of leadership.

Another similarity cinches the relationship between Exodus and Numbers. The same Hebrew root—'ṣl—occurs both in Numbers 11, when the elders of Israel accompany Moses in the desert, and in Exodus 24, when they accompany him up Mount Sinai. In Numbers 11:16–17, God promises to "take some of the spirit that is on" Moses; in Exodus 24:11, the same Hebrew root describes the elders ('ăṣîlê) who ascend Mount Sinai. There is, therefore, a taut relationship, in Hebrew, between the story of the elders who receive a share of the spirit that is on Moses (Num. 11) in the wilderness and the elders who climb Mount Sinai (Exod. 24).

What happened on Mount Sinai illuminates what happens in the desert when the spirit on Moses is distributed to the elders. Exodus 24 describes how Moses took seventy of the elders of Israel with him, along with Aaron, Nadab, and Abihu, up to Mount Sinai, where "they saw the God of Israel. Under his feet there was something like a pavement of sapphire stone, like the very heaven for clearness. God did not lay his hand on the chief men of the people of Israel; also they beheld God, and they ate and drank" (24:10–11). This story presents the seventy elders as participants with Moses in a visionary experience.

From this vantage point, Exodus 24 supplies what is implicit in the narrative of Numbers 11: prophesying consisted of a visionary experience, with an established social hierarchy and an appointed place of revelation. The elders earlier (Exod. 24) were appointed to bear Moses's burden with him by gathering at a place of revelation—Mount Sinai—and participating in a communal visionary experience alongside Moses. Later (Num. 11), the elders bear Moses's burden with him by gathering at another place of revelation—the tent of meeting—in order to function as the bearers of the spirit by participating in a communal visionary experience. This experience provides Moses with the backing he needs to lead the refractory Israelites to the promised land. Although the narrator does not disclose the contents of this vision, the association with Exodus 24 suggests that this experience led the elders, along with Moses, into a vision of God, not unlike the one at Mount Sinai, which was pivotal in supporting Moses. The sheer weight of a communal visionary experience, prompted by the distribution of the spirit that is upon him, underscores that Moses is not alone, that the elders bear the burden of the people with him.

The selection of the root *'ṣl*, in summary, to depict the drawing of the spirit from Moses, evokes the narrative in Exodus 24, according to which the seventy elders shared in a vision of God. From this perspective, prophesying in Numbers 11 consists of a vision—the contents of which are no longer entirely accessible to us—which enabled the elders to stand alongside Moses, to receive revelation in concert with Moses, and to bear with Moses the burden of carrying the Israelites.

There is, as there often is in the Old Testament, a surprising twist in the telling of this story. Two other elders, neither of them authorized by proximity to the tent of meeting, also participated in this vision. Eldad and Medad, who did not go with the others to the tent but remained in the camp, also prophesied. Joshua was alarmed, Moses elated. "Are you jealous for my sake?" asked Moses. "Would that all the LORD's people were prophets, and that the LORD would put his spirit on them!" (Num. 11:29). Here we see the contagion of the spirit, the uncontrollability, the ability of the spirit to blur the line between an established social hierarchy and a breach of propriety— a glimpse of the spirit we have seen time and again in other stories and sayings.

The Elders and the Messianic Ruler

If the *withdrawal* of the spirit from Moses is depicted by an evocative Hebrew root, *'ṣl*, the *conferral* of the spirit upon the elders is depicted by an equally significant root, *nûaḥ*, which we encountered already in Isaiah's portrait of the inspired ruler:

> The spirit of the LORD shall rest on[9] him,
>> the spirit of wisdom and understanding,
>> the spirit of counsel and might,
>> the spirit of knowledge and the fear of the LORD. (Isa. 11:2)

The quality of this leadership, we saw, is evident in justice for the poor, judgment of the wicked, righteousness and faithfulness, and, eventually, the restoration of Eden and the universal reign of Israel's ideal leader, despite the precarious political situation that confronted Israel.

The selection of the root *nûaḥ* in Numbers 11:25–26 to depict the presence of the spirit with the elders of Israel reflects a shared perspective with this prophetic image of an inspired ruler. Both have to do with charisma in its strongest sense—the messianic ruler's inspired leadership and the sharing of Moses's leadership with the elders. At the heart of each of these texts is capable, *inspired* leadership.

The root *nûaḥ* may offer an additional clue to inspiration in the story of the elders. Isaiah's description of the messianic ruler clearly implies that the restivng of the spirit is a permanent endowment. Perhaps this understanding of the verb *to rest* as a permanent en-

---

9. In 2 Kings 2, Elisha requests a double portion of Elijah's spirit. When Elijah ascends, Elisha picks up Elijah's mantle and successfully parts the Jordan River, as Elijah had, and walks from one side to the other. The narrative continues, "When the company of prophets who were at Jericho saw him at a distance, they declared, 'The spirit of Elijah rests on Elisha'" (2 Kings 2:15). In other words, they acknowledge the successful transference of Elijah's spirit to Elisha.

dowment prompted the narrator in Numbers 11:25 to append an otherwise odd sentence. "Then the LORD came down in the cloud and spoke to him, and took some of the spirit that was on him and put it on the seventy elders; and when the spirit rested upon them, they prophesied. *But they did not do so again*" (Num. 11:25). The elders did not prophesy again. In other words, their endowment was not permanent, despite the selection of the verb *to rest*, which would otherwise communicate a permanent endowment and a perpetual experience. Their ability to perceive God was transitory, the storyteller confirms, occasioned by Moses's request en route to the promised land for help in carrying his people.

———   ———   ———

We may now have solved the puzzle of the case of the inspired elders—how prophesying provided aid to a beleaguered Moses. Consideration of all three of the verbs that connect to the spirit in Numbers 11 suggests an experience that transcended any one of them taken in isolation.

The image of a group of elders engaged in prophesying certainly mirrors the experience of Saul, who prophesied in some sort of ecstasy in the company of a band of prophets. Saul's experiences were intense and communal, leading, in the first instance, to a transformation of Saul (1 Sam. 10:6–7) and in the last, to the question, Is Saul also among the prophets?

Yet this is not the whole of the experience of the elders. If we shrug off a fixation upon the verb *to prophesy* and consider two other verbs in Numbers 11, the picture shifts—and broadens. The verb *to withdraw* leads by association to Exodus 24 and the possibility that the elders' prophesying consisted of a visionary experience. The verb *to rest* leads by association to Isaiah 11, in which an inspired ruler, grounded in knowledge and justice, brings justice to the world. Understood afresh, the references to prophesying in Numbers 11 establish a clear relationship between the promise of the spirit and Moses's need of help to lead the people: Moses experienced God alongside, rather than in isolation from, a close coterie of leaders, whom the spirit inspired in the context of a communal visionary experience to aid Moses in his administrative responsibilities.

We can see in this story a creative amalgamation of traditions. The verb *to prophesy* connects the story of the elders to stories in which the spirit comes upon individual figures with drama and overt power—Balaam and Saul, in particular—and perhaps overcomes them. The verb *to rest* connects the story of the elders to a collection of texts that derive their inspiration from Isaiah 11. In these texts, the spirit does not overpower; the spirit inspires with knowledge, wisdom, and justice. Equally important is that the verb *take from* or *withdraw* recalls the story of Israel at Sinai, according to which the elders of Israel shared a remarkable visionary experience on the mountain. The spirit is able, in other words, to bring about Sinai in the desert. Unbounded by topography, untrammeled by landscape, even sacred landscape, the spirit moves as powerfully as at Sinai, not only among those commissioned and compliant, but even with a pair that, for reasons unknown, did not join the others near the sacred tent.

What is striking in this story is that this spirit can be withdrawn—siphoned off might be the right image—and made to rest on others. This is yet another vivid portrait of inspiration. It is idiosyncratic, too, as the spirit moves, in a sort of contagion, not just from one individual to another, like Moses to Joshua or Elijah to Elisha, but from one individual to many others, authorized or not.

Moses and Joshua

More poignant even than this realization is the image of Moses that caps this story of the inspired elders. Moses is magnanimous, open to the work of the spirit beyond his control: "Would that all the LORD's people were prophets, and that the LORD would put his spirit on them!" Moses is capable of *not* being in charge in the presence of the spirit. Small wonder, then, that he is described in his final hours as having undimmed eyes and a peculiar freshness so that, one last time, he could pass the spirit on, not to a host of elders but to one younger man, a protégé, whose impact would outstrip them all.

Joshua had accompanied Moses, fought in a valley while Moses prayed with hands propped up in prayer (Exod. 17:8–13), joined Moses at Mount Sinai and the tent of meeting (24:12–14; 33:11), even received a name Moses had given him (Num. 13:16). The gift of the spirit from Moses to Joshua is not surprising; it is so predictable, in fact, that it occurs in two versions. The authors of the books of Numbers and Deuteronomy both tell the story of how succession took place by the laying of Moses's hand upon Joshua, yet they tell the story differently.

When the time comes to appoint a successor, Moses favors Joshua, who has been his faithful protégé for years. "So the LORD said to Moses, 'Take Joshua son of Nun, a man in whom is [the] spirit, and lay your hand upon him; have him stand before Eleazar the priest and all the congregation, and commission him in their sight'" (Num. 27:18–19). Because of Joshua's abilities—the spirit is *already* in him—Moses lays his hand upon him to appoint him to lead Israel. This is one of those stories in the Old Testament into which it would be a mistake to introduce an artificial divide between the Spirit of God and the spirit-breath in Joshua. In this instance, *rûaḥ* is the source of Joshua's faithfulness, vitality, and loyalty. It is enough to say that Joshua has *rûaḥ* in him.

This understanding of the spirit is borne out by how it evokes the portrayal of Joseph, whom Pharaoh recognized as a person "in whom is the spirit of God" (Gen. 41:38). Joseph had led the ancestors of Israel through dire famine into a fertile land of promise. Joshua, who is similarly identified as one "in whom is (the) spirit," will lead the descendants of Joseph's family into another fertile land. The parallel between Joseph and Joshua is inescapable: both have *rûaḥ* in them.

Joshua does not in the book of Numbers receive a fresh endowment of the spirit—he already has spirit—but he does receive, along with the laying on of Moses's hand, a portion of Moses's magnificence, the sort of majesty that the psalmist consistently attributes to God and the sort of splendor that was, later in Israel's story, apportioned to kings.[10] God commands Moses, "You shall give him

10. For example, Job 40:10; Pss. 96:6; 104:1.

some of your *majesty*,[11] so that all the congregation of the Israelites may obey" (Num. 27:20). Moses also gives Joshua his final marching orders: "he laid his hands on him and commissioned him" (27:23). Joshua receives a great deal from Moses, including some of Moses's majesty and a final command. What he does *not* receive is a fresh endowment of the spirit. There is no transference of the spirit in the book of Numbers.

■ ■ ■

A briefer account of Joshua's commissioning occurs in Deuteronomy 34:9: "Joshua son of Nun was full of the spirit of wisdom, because Moses had laid his hands on him; and the Israelites obeyed him, doing as the LORD had commanded Moses." According to this account, Joshua did receive an infusion of *rûaḥ*. This influx of spirit is directly tied to Moses's laying on of hands, though the laying on of hands does not generate dramatic abilities in Joshua. From this point on, in fact, nothing occurs automatically for Joshua because he has a spirit of wisdom, which he received from the laying on of Moses's hands. He tears apart no lions, participates in no prophesying, slays no giants. Despite the laying on of Moses's hands, absolutely nothing Joshua accomplishes can be unequivocally attributed to the spirit in him.

From here on out, Joshua's wisdom is the product of dogged effort. The early lines in the book that bears his name indicate as much: "Only be strong and very courageous, being careful to act in accordance with all the law that my servant Moses commanded you; do not turn from it to the right hand or to the left, so that you may be successful wherever you go. This book of the law shall not depart out of your mouth; you shall meditate on it day and night, so that you may be careful to act in accordance with all that is written in it. For then you shall make your way prosperous, and then you shall be successful" (Josh. 1:7–8). Wisdom is tethered directly to the study of Torah. If Joshua is to conquer and divide the promised land, he must possess intimate knowledge of the instructions for distributing the land in the book of Numbers. If, then, Deuteronomy 34:9 depicts an

11. NRSV "authority."

endowment with the spirit of wisdom, it is one that is accompanied by strict instructions about meditation upon written words. There is no dichotomy between a full endowment of the spirit of wisdom and scrupulous attention to the Torah. They are joined at the hip.

Lying beneath this passing of the spirit in Deuteronomy 34:9 is Moses's palpable vitality. "Moses was one hundred twenty years old when he died; his sight was *not dimmed* and his *freshness* was not gone" (Deut. 34:7 alt.). The word *freshness* usually occurs with plants: fresh grapes in contrast to dried (Num. 6:3); the green or fresh tree as opposed to the dry (Ezek. 17:24); the fresh cords that tied Samson down (Judg. 16:7–8). This is a subtle but sparkling tribute to Moses, who, after decades of discouragement and bouts of exhaustion, still possessed a vitality of the spirit that he could pass on to Joshua through physical contact—the laying on of hands. Having given his life to a community of refugees, Moses was still fresh, still green, still alive, capable of imparting, one last time, a spirit of wisdom to his friend and faithful protégé.

Elijah and Elisha

Like Joshua, the prophet Elisha was a serious and reliable protégé who would not let loose his mentor. So intertwined were they that other prophets referred to Elijah as *Elisha's* master rather than their own (2 Kings 2:3, 5). Elijah was certainly a worthy mentor. A man of miracles, he multiplied meal and oil (1 Kings 17:8–16), raised a widow's son from the dead (17:17–24), called rain and fire from heaven (18:38, 41–46), parted the waters of the Jordan River (2 Kings 2:8), and accurately predicted Jezebel's gruesome death (9:30–37).

Elijah, a prophet in the Northern Kingdom during the ninth century BCE, receives more play in the book of 1 Kings than any of Israel's kings. *His* story is the backbone of the biblical story. The kernel of his work can be summed up in a single encounter with Ahab, king of Israel. When Ahab sees Elijah, who is responsible for a protracted drought, Ahab says, "Is it you, you troubler of Israel?" (1 Kings 18:17). The word *troubler* is too soft. *Destroyer* is no doubt better.[12] The king views Elijah as the destroyer of Israel. Elijah, of course, prophet that he is, sets the record straight: "I have not troubled Israel; but you have, and your father's house, because you have forsaken the commandments of the LORD and followed the Baals" (18:18).

Elijah was known as a man of the spirit, though in a less conventional way than someone like Joshua. For example, Elijah knew a man named Obadiah, a high-ranking member of Queen Jezebel and King Ahab's court. Obadiah was sympathetic to prophets like Elijah, who opposed the king and queen; Obadiah had even hidden a hundred of them when Jezebel tried to kill them. In a chance encounter, Elijah told Obadiah to tell King Ahab that Elijah was there. Obadiah responded, first in horror at handing Elijah over to the king, and then with this thought: "As soon as I have gone from you, the *rûaḥ* of the LORD will carry you I know not where; so, when I come and tell Ahab and he cannot find you, he will kill me, although I your servant have revered the LORD from my youth" (1 Kings 18:12). Not so much the spirit of God *within* Elijah as the wind-spirit able to transport him—this is the operative, slightly unconventional mode of inspiration in this story. Then, after his being taken up in a chariot, the coterie of prophets left behind went to search for him, so they said to Elisha, "See now, we have fifty strong men among your servants; please let them go and seek your master; it may be that the *rûaḥ* of the LORD has caught him up and thrown him down on some mountain or into some valley" (2 Kings 2:16). Once again, the spirit does not so much indwell Elijah as subsume him, not so much fill as surround him.

Rûaḥ plays a role, too, in the story of how Elijah brought an end to the years-long drought, which King Ahab pinned on him. In a public confrontation with four hundred prophets of Baal, whom Jezebel employed, Elijah triumphed. The end arrived when "in a little while the heavens grew black with clouds and *rûaḥ*; there was a heavy rain" (1 Kings 18:45). This *rûaḥ* is wind, of course, but wind that moves at God's—and Elijah's—bidding. Elijah is a man of the spirit, but again, not in a conventional way.

12. The Hebrew word *'āḳar* is used in this sense in Gen. 34:30; Josh. 6:18; 7:25.

After this confrontation, Elijah lost his nerve. In a spasm of weakness, he retreated from Jezebel to a cave at Mount Sinai in an apparent effort to repeat Moses's experience on the same mountain. He stood at the mouth of the cave. "Now there was a great *rûaḥ*, so strong that it was splitting mountains and breaking rocks in pieces before the LORD, but the LORD was not in the *rûaḥ*; and after the *rûaḥ* an earthquake, but the LORD was not in the earthquake; and after the earthquake a fire, but the LORD was not in the fire; and after the fire a sound of sheer silence" (1 Kings 19:11–12). God is no longer in the phenomena that had attended Israel's sojourn at Sinai, when the awesome mountain had quaked and ignited (Exod. 19–24).

This shift from theophany to absence is stunning, particularly in light of Elijah's storied prophetic activity. In the course of Elijah's life, God was in the spirit-wind, as at the end of the drought or in the specter of spectacular transport—but not now, when he, cowed by his queen, retreats to Mount Sinai. The absence of activity associated with this *rûaḥ* in Elijah's lifetime is conspicuous. Now, rather than receiving divine direction, Elijah hears nothing in the *rûaḥ* except the sound of silence. What he does hear marks the end of his prophetic activity. He is told to appoint a successor, a new king over Syria, and a new king over the Northern Kingdom. He is, in short, to prepare the next generation, in which he will not take part. His protégé will.

Toward the end of Elijah's life, Elisha begs Elijah for a double share of his spirit. Elijah does not respond as Moses did, with a peaceful transferal of the spirit. Instead, he tells Elisha, "You have asked a hard thing; yet, if you see me as I am being taken from you, it will be granted you; if not, it will not" (2 Kings 2:10). This may be one last challenge, one final lesson to test the tenacity of his protégé—something Moses had not done to Joshua.

Of course, Elisha is nothing if not tenacious, so he does see Elijah taken away in a fiery chariot. When he does, he grips his own garment, tearing it in two, then picks up Elijah's characteristic furry mantle and divides the Jordan River with it, just as Elijah had done moments earlier (2 Kings 2:8, 13–14). This elicits a telling response from the prophets around him: "The spirit of Elijah rests on Elisha" (2 Kings 2:9–15). This is the same verb, *rest*, used to describe the inspiration of the messianic ruler in Isaiah's vision (Isa. 11:2) and the resting of the spirit on the elders in the wilderness (Num. 11:25). It marks a permanent endowment, a source of wisdom and a reign in which even animals become docile. For Elisha, as for Elijah, even the natural world bows its knee to the one on whom the spirit rests.

This is a strange rather than straightforward story. It is not at all clear why Elisha demands a double portion of Elijah's spirit when a single portion will do. Nor is it clear why Elijah stipulates that Elisha must see the ascent of the chariot if he is to inherit the spirit. It is not clear what the relationship is—there seems to be some sort of relationship—between Elijah's furry mantle and the gift of the spirit. None of this is clear; all of it is perplexing. Yet one dimension is sure: the spirit passes from mentor to protégé. This is clear. This is not perplexing. Capable mentors transfer skill and knowledge and wisdom to faithful protégés, some of whom, like Elijah's Elisha, prove trustworthy, and others of whom, like Elisha's Gehazi,[13] prove unreliable.

The passing on of the spirit, therefore, is neither incomprehensible nor automatic. It demands loyalty, learning, and trust on the part of both mentor and protégé. Moses had to trust Joshua, whether his protégé was fighting in a valley or waiting at the foot of a mountain. Elijah had to trust Elisha, who was tenacious in his effort to accompany his mentor. And the protégés had to trust their mentors. In the bonds of this trust, the spirit passed from mentor to protégé, from teacher to student, from old to young. The taut relationships in these stories make it possible to muse not only on whether the protégé matured in the presence of the mentor (this seems inevitable) but also on whether these relationships kept the mentor young, vibrant, and fresh, like Moses, whose eyes were undimmed and whose vitality was still fresh, or Elijah, who could put his protégé to the test one last time before rising spectacularly in a chariot of fire—though not without leaving behind a furry mantle for his determined young friend, who picked it up and, of course, mirrored the master.

---

13. The story of Gehazi, a less than ideal figure who serves Elisha, is found in 2 Kings 4–8.

5

Spirit Poured Out

Before reading this chapter, explore these texts:

>> Isaiah 32:9–20
>> Isaiah 44:1–5
>> Ezekiel 39:17–29
>> Joel 2:23–3:3
>> Zechariah 12:1–13:6

When the prophet Ezekiel, in the throes of exile, launches an image of hope, he does so by constructing a new temple in the imaginations of refugees from Judah now barely subsisting in Babylon. Their own temple is in ruins, so Ezekiel describes, in excruciating detail, cubit by cubit, a new temple. Flowing from beneath this ideal temple, which exists now only in Ezekiel's imagination, is a river. His guide on this imaginary journey, "going on eastward with a cord in his hand," recalls Ezekiel, "measured one thousand cubits, and then led me through the water; and it was ankle-deep. Again he measured one thousand, and led me through the water; and it was knee-deep. Again he measured one thousand, and led me through the water; and it was up to the waist. Again he measured one thousand, and it was a river that I could not cross, for the water had risen; it was deep enough to swim in, a river that could not be crossed. He said to me, 'Mortal, have you seen this?'" (Ezek. 47:3–6). Of course, Ezekiel had not seen it; no one had. Yet it is lavish—ankle-deep water eventually becoming uncrossable.

Then, while walking along the riverbank, recalls Ezekiel, "I saw on the bank of the river a great many trees on the one side and on the other" (Ezek. 47:7). Ezekiel's image is dramatic, illusory even, the topography of restoration rather than reality. Yet it shares with the first poem in Israel's psalter a sense of the importance of water—trees planted alongside water flourish. "They are like trees planted by streams of water, which yield their fruit in its season, and their leaves do not wither. In all that they do, they prosper" (Ps. 1:3). These are the students, the learners, who meditate night and day on Torah. In a topography prone to drought, with two seasons and two seasons only—wet and dry, hot and cool—there can be no more apt an image of dedication than trees planted by streams of water, yielding fruit in season and out, year after year, decade by decade.

Ezekiel shares this vision of fidelity with his near contemporary Jeremiah, a more practical and less quixotic soul than Ezekiel. "Blessed are those who trust in the LORD, whose trust is the LORD," utters Jeremiah. "They shall be like a tree planted by water, sending out its roots by the stream. It shall not fear when heat comes, and its leaves shall stay green; in the year of drought it is not anxious, and it does not cease to bear fruit" (Jer. 17:7–8).

Water. In the topography of Palestine, ancient and modern, water is of the essence. Lack of water is death, a cursed desert. That is why Jeremiah contrasts the blessed—trees planted by flowing rivers— with the cursed, those "who trust in mere mortals and make mere flesh their strength, whose hearts turn away from the Lord." These, Jeremiah knows, "shall be like a shrub in the desert, and shall not see when relief comes. They shall live in the parched places of the wilderness, in an uninhabited salt land" (Jer. 17:5–6).

To the author of Deuteronomy, like Jeremiah, drought is the essence of curse, which is depicted with perturbing but not unrealistic images: "The LORD will afflict you with consumption, fever, inflammation, with fiery heat and drought, and with blight and mildew; they shall pursue you until you perish. The sky over your head shall be bronze, and the earth under you iron. The LORD will change the rain of your land into powder, and only dust shall come down upon you from the sky until you are destroyed" (Deut. 28:22–24). Powder. Dust. Bronze. Iron. *Drought.*

The prophet Amos complains that Israel fails to see the significance of drought. "I gave you cleanness of teeth in all your cities, and lack of bread in all your places, yet you did not return to me," complains Amos's God. "And I also withheld the rain from you when there were still three months to the harvest; I would send rain on one city, and send no rain on another city; one field would be rained upon, and the field on which it did not rain withered; so two or three towns wandered to one town to drink water, and were not satisfied; yet you did not return to me, says the LORD" (Amos 4:6–8). Failing to grasp the cursed state they are in, they are destined finally to fail—which Israel did, just three decades after Amos decried their injustice.

Drought can also express deep personal alienation. "O God, you are my God, I seek you, my soul thirsts for you," confesses one of Israel's poets. "My flesh faints for you, as in a dry and weary land where there is no water" (Ps. 63:1).

Water. Water is plush, lush, green, and growing. Even in a book such as Leviticus, often more prosaic than prophetic, God waxes eloquent about water as a reward for faithfulness: "If you follow my statutes and keep my commandments and observe them faithfully, I will give you your rains in their season, and the land shall yield its produce, and the trees of the field shall yield their fruit. Your threshing shall overtake the vintage, and the vintage shall overtake the sowing; you shall eat your bread to the full, and live securely in your land" (Lev. 26:3–5). The book of Deuteronomy thrums with similar tones: "If you will only heed his every commandment that I am commanding you today—loving the LORD your God, and serving him with all your heart and with all your soul—then he will give the rain for your land in its season, the early rain and the later rain, and you will gather in your grain, your wine, and your oil; and he will give grass in your fields for your livestock, and you will eat your fill" (11:13–15).[1]

1. Solomon, in his prayer at the dedication of the temple, recognizes the relationship between sin and drought, penitence and plenty: "When heaven is shut up and there is no rain because they have sinned against you, and then they pray toward this

The step from an outburst of rain to an outpouring of the spirit is a small one, little more than a jig or a jog, very nearly just a sidestep. Both are the quintessence of blessing. Both prompt transformation. Both bring growth and health and vitality in their train.

In the course of several centuries, therefore, Israel's prophets imagined the spirit outpoured to be a source of transformation. Whether during times of political uncertainty or decades of sheer anguish, Israel's prophets looked ahead to the spirit outpoured, refreshing nature (Isa. 32:15–20), turning God's people into a green tree in a vast desert (Isa. 44:3–4), bringing Israel home (Ezek. 36–39), transforming slave girls into prophets (Joel 2:28–29; MT 3:1–2), and evoking unprecedented remorse in the wake of political violence (Zech. 12:10). Though all of these imaginings are unique—each has its own geopolitical context, its own emphasis, its own hue—common to all of them, which span from the eighth to the fifth century BCE or later, is the conviction that the spirit outpoured is sheer blessing, even when that blessing brings a jarring metamorphosis in society's otherwise settled norms.[2]

Fruitful Fields

Like prophets through the ages, Isaiah is apoplectic because those around him fail to see the signs of the times. Not just politicians, Isaiah realizes, but the leading women of Jerusalem are complicit in complacency. They are *at ease, confident,* and *all too trusting.* Like Amos, Zechariah, Job, and the psalmist, Isaiah vilifies those who are

---

place, confess your name, and turn from their sin, because you punish them, then hear in heaven, and forgive the sin of your servants, your people Israel, when you teach them the good way in which they should walk; and grant rain on your land, which you have given to your people as an inheritance" (1 Kings 8:35–36). Drought even moves the story of Israel along in its treacherous wake. Abraham, Isaac, and Jacob had to move because of famines in the wake of drought (Gen. 12; 26; 41). In Egypt, Joseph rose up through the ranks because he managed a protracted drought (Gen. 41). Elijah staved off the death of a widow in Zarephath during a period of extended drought (1 Kings 17:7–24), which concluded in a dramatic confrontation with the prophets of Baal on Mount Carmel (18:1–46).

2. In Isa. 29:10, God pours out a spirit of deep sleep upon the prophets, Judah's seers.

at ease, who cannot fathom that misfortune will catch up to them.[3] It will; misfortune will overtake them. Still, they are altogether overly confident—Isaiah calls them this three times in quick succession (Isa. 32:9–11)—happily going about life without a sense of their impending doom.[4] Perhaps the political alliances that are in place give these women a false sense of security; Isaiah time and again calls these alliances into question, especially with Egypt as a buffer against the growing threat of Assyrian invasion. The women, though, do not see the threat, so they go about their business with misplaced trust.

These women, Isaiah urges, should beat their breasts in funerary mourning for the soon-to-come death of their fields and vines. They should tremble, shudder, strip, put on sackcloth, and beat their breasts in mourning for pleasant fields and jubilant houses, "for the palace will be forsaken, the populous city deserted; the hill and the watchtower will become dens forever, the joy of wild asses, a pasture for flocks" (Isa. 32:14).

Until. The women should mourn

> until a spirit from on high is poured out on us,
>   and the wilderness becomes a fruitful field,
>   and the fruitful field is deemed a forest.
>
> Then justice will dwell in the wilderness,
>   and righteousness abide in the fruitful field.
> The effect of righteousness will be peace,
>   and the result of righteousness, quietness and trust
>   forever.
> My people will abide in a peaceful habitation,
>   in secure dwellings, and in quiet resting places.
>   (Isa. 32:15–18)

It is not entirely clear how proper judgment will dwell in the wilderness and justice in fruitful fields. Perhaps landowners—the women's husbands—will finally act in justice toward workers and tenant

---

3. Amos 6:1; Zech. 1:15; Job 12:5; Ps. 123:4.

4. NRSV translates the Hebrew *bōṭḥôt* as "complacent," which fails to capture the sense of trust inherent in this word. "Overly confident" and "all too trusting" are better, if clumsier, translations.

farmers. Perhaps they will leave the corners of their fields unharvested so that the poor and aliens, like Ruth and Naomi, can gather their food. Still, inchoate as this promise is, it offers an expansive image: both wilderness and cultivated fields will be the locus of the spirit's deluge.

Water. We come back to the blessing of water. Like water, the spirit will be outpoured, turning deserts into fields and fields into forests. Yet this word *outpoured*,[5] while it can be used of emptying a jar (Gen. 24:20), is also used of *laying bare* or *exposing*. For instance, Isaiah predicts that "the LORD will afflict with scabs the heads of the daughters of Zion, and the Lord will *lay bare* their secret parts" (Isa. 3:17). No doubt outpouring in Isaiah's oracle is just that: the spirit will be poured out like a heavy rain. But in the background lies, too, the laying bare of the women in Jerusalem, who should strip and wear sackcloth but who will not do so, not of their own doing at least. Only calamity and chaos will cause them to beat their—now exposed—breasts.

This is the cycle Isaiah envisions: destruction followed by restoration. In both desert, where Israel once wandered, and cultivated field, where they now live, there will be justice. The residue of right judgment and justice will be peace, quietness, lack of fear, security, and stability. In the aftermath of destruction, in the wake of desolation, when the spirit is poured out, the people will come home.

Restoration

More than a century later, as exile strangled Judah, Ezekiel sprang into motion with a quick succession of promises. He promised, first, the gift of a new heart and spirit: "A new heart I will give you, and a new spirit I will put within you; and I will remove from your body the heart of stone and give you a heart of flesh. I will put my spirit within you, and make you follow my statutes and be careful to observe my ordinances" (Ezek. 36:26–27). He promised, second, in a magnificent vision, that God would breathe new life into very many, very dry bones (37:1–14). This extraordinary vision is capped with

5. Hebrew root, *'rh*.

the promise, "I will put my spirit within you, and you shall live, and I will place you on your own soil; then you shall know that I, the Lord, have spoken and will act, says the Lord" (37:14). In still a third promise, Ezekiel predicts that the restored nation will "know that I am the Lord their God because I sent them into exile among the nations, and then gathered them into their own land. I will leave none of them behind; and I will never again hide my face[6] from them, when I pour out my spirit upon the house of Israel, says the Lord God" (39:28–29).

Ezekiel's bold claim that exile will end when the spirit is outpoured, though novel, is not surprising. The outpouring of rain brings an end to drought; the outpouring of the spirit will bring an end to exile. The parallel is obvious.

The meaning of Ezekiel's claim that God will not hide God's presence-face is less obvious because it requires awareness of a tortured negotiation that took place between God and Moses on Mount Sinai (Exod. 33). Two issues were at stake in that protracted and painful negotiation. First was *whether* God would accompany only Moses or Israel as a whole to the promised land; God and Moses seem to have disagreed on this point, with God refusing to accompany Israel as a whole but happy to accompany Moses. Second was *who* would accompany Israel or Moses—an angel or God's presence-face. Again, God and Moses disagreed on this point, with God refusing to show even Moses the divine face. No one could see God's face and live—not even Moses (Exod. 33:20–23). God's glory, yes, Moses could see, at least from the rear. But not God's face. Never.

Ezekiel's promise resolves both tensions in this tense negotiation. When the spirit is outpoured, God will accompany the entire house of Israel, not just Moses, on their return to their homeland. Plus all Israel—not just Moses, whose request God had denied long ago on Mount Sinai—will see God's presence-face. Against the background of the negotiation between God and Moses, Ezekiel's promise is explosive, signaling a divine turnaround. It is not just a prediction of restoration to their homeland; it promises restoration of relationship

6. The Hebrew noun (without the Hebrew suffix "my") is *pānîm*, which I translate as "presence-face." See chap. 1 n. 13.

with God. And all of this will happen when God pours out God's spirit on Israel.

Fresh Descendants

Decades after Ezekiel issued his astonishing series of promises—a new heart and spirit, new life blown into desiccated bones, and the end of divine hiddenness with the spirit outpoured—they remained unfulfilled. This state of affairs did not prevent another prophet, this one in the line of Isaiah, from promising the spirit outpoured to men and women in exile. Yet the situation had changed with the decades that had passed since the early days of exile, which people like Ezekiel endured. Shifts in international politics had an almost immediate impact upon the Judean exiles in Babylon. The great empire of Babylon fell to Persia, whose policy was not exile of the vanquished but a return of the conquered to their homelands. In light of the rise of Persia, hope burgeoned, at least for this prophet, and anticipation mushroomed into a promise of spectacular proportions:

> But now hear, O Jacob my servant,
>   Israel whom I have chosen!
> Thus says the LORD who made you,
>   who formed you in the womb and will help you:
> Do not fear, O Jacob my servant,
>   Jeshurun whom I have chosen.
> For I will pour water on the thirsty land,
>   and streams on the dry ground;
> I will pour my spirit upon your descendants,
>   and my blessing on your offspring.
> They shall spring up like a green tamarisk,
>   like willows by flowing streams.
> This one will say, "I am the LORD's,"
>   another will be called by the name of Jacob,
> yet another will write on the hand, "The LORD's,"
>   and adopt the name of Israel. (Isa. 44:1–5)

Israel, whom the prophet identifies as God's servant—a cherished epithet for a people long exiled—has suffered enough; they are now in desperate need of hope. This promise, therefore, is framed to allay fear: the promise to descendants and offspring recalls the promised blessing to Abraham and Sarah of many descendants, like the sand on the seashore and the stars in heaven.[7] This is not an entirely new promise; it is a *renewed* promise. From smallness comes national prominence. From insignificance arises a great people. From an exilic few rises a national many.

There is a baseline to this promise. There *will be* descendants. There *will be* offspring. Deportation is not so dire, exile so awful, that Abraham and Sarah's family will expire or be expunged from history. This in itself is grounds for hope.

Yet there may be something fresh here. While the prophet envisions a rekindling of Israel's fidelity, the prophet's promise that some will write on their hands "The LORD's" and be called by the name of Israel may refer to foreigners who pledge fidelity to Israel. The hope of Judah in this promise may rest not merely in the replenishment of Israel's numbers, of Abraham and Sarah's physical descendants, but in the future work of the spirit among those who have not yet professed their faith in the God of Abraham and Sarah. The verb translated "adopt" occurs slightly later in a depiction of a beneficent—in the prophet's estimate, at least—foreigner, the Persian ruler Cyrus: "For the sake of my servant Jacob, and Israel my chosen, I call you by your name, I *name* you, though you do not know me" (Isa. 45:4, italics added). God, in short, claims Cyrus as God's own. God *adopts* him. It is possible, in this light, that the writing of God's name on a hand and being named with the name of Israel together refer to new members of Judah, to those who are not natural-born citizens but daughters and sons adopted by an expansive God. This too is the effect of the outpouring of the spirit.

The untamed torrents of the spirit, then, may not be contained within Judah's family tree; they overflow to a world that has yet to profess faith in Israel's God—including, just a few strophes later, Cyrus of Persia. This is a remarkable response to Israel's situation. Although Babylon had nearly extinguished this small nation, the nation's future lies in the spirit's ability to renew and refresh so that believers from

7. E.g., Gen. 12:3; 22:17–18; 26:4.

other nations will willingly enslave themselves to Israel's God, writing on their hands "The LORD's" and adopting the name of Israel.

Whether it includes only Abraham and Sarah's physical descendants or new citizens of Israel from other nations, the lavishness of this exilic promise contrasts with the earlier promise of Isaiah 32:15. In the eighth-century promise, Isaiah chose a verb with the nuance of laying bare, which connotes by extension the sense of emptying: the spirit will be emptied onto the wilderness. The verb in the exilic prophecy (Isa. 44:3) communicates outpouring, such as of oil for anointing, water for cleansing or washing, and blood for sacrifices. This lavishness is especially accented by the presence of torrents in the desert: water on thirsty ground, torrents on dry ground. The shift from laying bare (32:15) to outpouring (44:3) matches the more drastic situation of exile. No more is Judah in a state of mere political angst; now Judah has lost land, king, and temple. The wilderness is not just imminent; the wilderness is, and has been for decades, here. The desert is all around this bereft and beleaguered people. If Abraham and Sarah's descendants are to survive, the outpouring must be full and final. They cannot hang on half-heartedly or grow desultorily in the hot sun; if they are to survive exile, return home, and rebuild Jerusalem, they must spring up like a green tamarisk, like willows by flowing streams.

Dreams and Visions

Israel's prophets could run wild with the spirit, though they never strayed far from their traditions. This tension between tradition and imagination finds expression in the book of Joel, where we encounter once again the outpouring of the spirit in a message that is of a piece with Isaiah's hope for the restoration of desolate cities (Isa. 32:15); with Ezekiel's deep longing, expressed in nationalistic and land-based terms, that God will be present to Israel—face-to-face—as never before (Ezek. 39:28–29); and with an exilic prophet's anticipation of renewed vitality for Israel, perhaps through the ingathering of foreigners (Isa. 44:3). Along the same vein, Joel imagines an indistinct day in the future:

> Then afterward
> I will pour out my spirit on all flesh;

> your sons and your daughters shall prophesy,
>> your old men shall dream dreams,
>> and your young men shall see visions.
> Even on the male and female slaves,
>> in those days, I will pour out my spirit.

> I will show portents in the heavens and on the earth, blood and fire
> and columns of smoke. The sun shall be turned to darkness, and the
> moon to blood, before the great and terrible day of the LORD comes.
> (Joel 2:28–31; MT 3:1–4)

This unbridled promise leaps out of the book of Joel. Nothing elsewhere in the book of Joel rises to this level of noteworthiness; elsewhere in the book, devastation is rife, lament formulaic, and promise
predictable.[8] There is little to excite the imagination—until, that is,
this promise of the outpouring of the spirit.

The object of outpouring, *all flesh*, outstrips all other Israelite conceptions of outpouring. In other prophetic texts, the spirit restores
Israel, propels foreigners to join Israel, and promises restoration of
the land to Israel. Joel envisages the scope of the spirit to include
all flesh. Yet here we may need to take a step back. In the context of
the book of Joel, *all flesh* would seem to mean all *Israelite* flesh. The
prophecy concludes with a battle in the valley of Jehoshaphat and
with Judah established in Jerusalem, surrounded by mountains that
drip sweet wine and hills from which flows milk. This is a pro-Judah
vision of the future.

In this particular promise of the spirit, however, no such limitation
is apparent, and the unspecified introduction "afterward" suggests
that Joel will not be pinned down to a historical fulfillment with
specific nations. Unlike Ezekiel, he will not anchor outpouring of the
spirit to a national restoration. Even the words *all flesh*, which can
be taken at face value to include animals (e.g., Gen. 6:19), usually
encompass all humankind.[9] This dream, this vision, extends to the
flesh of old and young, women and men—even to the flesh of slaves.

---

8. God will remove an unspecified northern army (Joel 2:20), give early and late
rains (2:23–24), repay Israel with food for years of a locust plague (2:26), and dwell
in Israel's midst, so that the people will never be put to shame (2:26–27).

9. E.g., Gen. 6:12; Deut. 5:26; Ps. 65:2; Isa. 49:26; 66:23.

What underlies this unexpected glimmer of universality is, surprisingly, the scenario of Moses and the elders, when Joshua claimed that two elders, Eldad and Medad, ought not to be allowed to prophesy because they failed to join the authorized seventy elders at the tent of meeting outside the camp. Moses responded to Joshua with words that could be translated word for word as "Are you jealous for my sake? Now who will give all the LORD's people to be prophets, for the LORD will give his spirit on them?" (Num. 11:29, my translation). Moses is exuberant in his desire that *everyone* in Israel should prophesy.

Now, in Joel's imagination, they do. How different this is from the story of Moses and the elders, when only *elders* prophesy. These are sanctioned male authorities in Israel; they alone receive the spirit from Moses in order to experience a vision that underwrites their authority to lead the nation alongside Moses. This auspicious circle disappears in Joel's transformation of this story, in which the spirit is poured out just as richly upon female slaves as upon elders. Even the words, *pour out my spirit*, are repeated for emphasis at the vision's beginning and end; the first to receive the spirit are sons, the last are female slaves. There is no trickling down of the spirit here.

In a book that otherwise travels a time-honored path, this outpouring of the spirit is extraordinary. The inclusion of slaves devastates the rule of order. So too does the inclusion of women, of daughters and female slaves. In this respect, Joel has stepped well beyond the boundaries of his tradition. We are no longer dealing with respectable men, such as Joseph, Moses, Joshua, Gideon, Micah, the ideal ruler, or the servant figure, or even men of questionable integrity, such as Balaam, Jephthah, Samson, or Saul. The spirit now is promised to women, and women of the lowest rank.

This outpouring is not just a simple reordering of society, though it is that. This is not a redistribution of wealth, though it may be that. Nor does it only wrest authority from people who are privileged by dint of age or gender, though it certainly does that. The outpouring of the spirit is also cataclysmic, part and parcel of "portents in the heavens and on the earth, blood and fire and columns of smoke," when "the sun shall be turned to darkness, and the moon to blood, before the great and terrible day of the LORD comes." This outpouring, though more dramatic and ominous, shares with Isaiah's vision of the inspired ruler (Isa. 11) the expectation of an era when the tilt of the world will shift, when its arc will bend toward justice—not in one slow, steady evolution but in a cataclysm. Nothing less will do, Joel knows, because the likelihood that human beings will listen freely and generously to the prophetic voices of men and women who are, and who always will be, their servants and slaves is just as small— perhaps smaller—as the likelihood that blood will appear in the sky. This listening—the swell of those voices—will happen not drop by measured drop but with a deluge of spirit poured out on all flesh.

Grief and Remorse

If the prophecy in Joel is striking for its largesse, a prophecy in the book of Zechariah[10] is salient for its specificity.

> And I will pour out a spirit of compassion and supplication on the house of David and the inhabitants of Jerusalem, so that, when they look on the one whom they have stabbed, they shall mourn for him, as one mourns for an only child, and weep bitterly over him, as one weeps over a firstborn. (Zech. 12:10)[11]

10. The passage discussed here in the book of Zechariah occurs in the final six chapters of the book, which may have been originally separate from and later than the first eight chapters. Carol and Eric Meyers offer an extensive discussion of this issue in *Zechariah 9–14: A New Translation with Introduction and Commentary*, Anchor Bible 25C (New York: Doubleday, 1993), 15–45.

11. Whether this has to do with the spirit of God or merely means that God will pour out a disposition, a *sense* of compassion and supplication, upon certain people is a moot point. The division between disposition or inspiration, human and divine spirit, attitude or possession, is one that does not rise readily to the surface of the literature of ancient Israel. For example, if a wife is sexually unfaithful to her husband but undetected, "if a spirit of jealousy comes on him, and he is jealous of his wife who has defiled herself; or if a spirit of jealousy comes on him, and he is jealous of his wife, though she has not defiled herself; then the man shall bring his wife to the priest" (Num. 5:14–15). The priest then subjects her to an awful test, in which she drinks the grain offering, and if her womb drops, she is considered guilty. Is the spirit of jealousy an actual spirit that possesses the husband, or is this an expression for a jealous state? The story of Saul, in which an evil spirit from God torments him and causes him to rage against David, may indicate belief in actual possession. Still, if the spirit of jealousy comes from God, why does the priest need to test the wife? Is the presence of a spirit of jealousy not enough? Another example of this ambiguity—or

This is a powerful prediction rooted in a violent act of stabbing and rife with the language of grief. At the opposite end of the spectrum from Joel, the recipients of this outpouring are limited to a small slice of humanity, to the house of David and the inhabitants of Jerusalem. Maids and butlers are nowhere in view. A subsequent list of mourners (Zech. 12:12–14) suggests who will receive this outpouring: the house of David (royalty), the house of Nathan (perhaps David's court prophet), and the house of Levi (priests and Levites). Therefore, this is not a sweeping outpouring; it is limited to elite groups. It is unlike the outpouring that will cause justice to dwell in the wilderness (Isa. 32:15–20), the outpouring that will come in torrents and initiate an influx of citizens (Isa. 44:3–5), the outpouring upon all flesh that will reach from elders to female slaves (Joel 2:28–32). This is a constricted outpouring of a spirit of compassion and supplication upon a particular group of privileged people who are responsible for a violent act of stabbing.

Constricted—but not insignificant. Enormous shifts in the tectonic plates of life in Jerusalem result from this outpouring. The spirit will instigate compassion or favor; the houses of David, Nathan, and Levi, in other words, will replace violence with favor. As a consequence, the houses of David, Nathan, and Levi will seek forgiveness from the one whom they stabbed. These perpetrators of evil will be utterly overcome by grief; the Hebrew verb translated "mourn" or "grieve" occurs no less than three times in this brief set of sayings, while the power of grief is expressed twice by the objects of grief: an only child, a firstborn. Utter desolation. Utter grief.

No doubt the verb *pour out*, which occurs as well in the promises of Ezekiel 39:28–29 and Joel 2:28–31, finds a haunting resonance in the

---

perhaps multivalence—of the notion of the spirit when it is attached to another noun (spirit of compassion and supplication, spirit of jealousy) is the description of an ideal ruler in Isa. 28:5–6: "In that day the Lord of hosts will be a garland of glory, and a diadem of beauty, to the remnant of his people; and a spirit of justice to the one who sits in judgment, and strength to those who turn back the battle at the gate." This text portrays God as a garland and a diadem, strength to warriors. Is the "spirit of justice" also a metaphor, or is this description to be understood in light of Isa. 11:1–6, in which the spirit seems to be a presence that endows the ideal ruler with virtues such as wisdom and knowledge? It is extremely difficult, perhaps impossible, to decide, nor is it necessarily desirable or responsible to decide, given the richness of the notion of *rûaḥ* in antiquity.

promise of Zechariah because typically it describes the shedding—
the outpouring—of blood in violent acts. In the sacrifice of animals,
blood is shed or poured out. More menacing, this verb is used of
illicit—*criminal*—acts of murder.[12] It is more than a little ironic that
a verb used to describe the shedding of blood in murder is used in
Zechariah to describe the outpouring of the spirit in reconciliation
following a violent stabbing.

As in the book of Joel, the timing of this prediction, "on that day,"
is vague. Nonetheless, what gives this text a force that may extend
beyond other visions of outpouring is its specificity. The promises
of Isaiah, Ezekiel, Isaiah of the exile, and Joel are magnificent, but
this prediction, more than the others, is rooted in an actual political
event: a violent, vile act of stabbing. This is no vision of lions and
lambs lying at peace together or of tamarisks sprouting in a renewed
desert; it evokes no imagined world where slaveowners regard their
slaves as prophets. This is a vision in which violent politicians, priests,
and court prophets are moved by unalloyed grief to embrace a former
opponent against whom they have acted with unspeakable violence.
Precisely because this vision is about actual politics and politicians,
the force of God's spirit poured out, a spirit that effects a complete
turnaround, that encloses whole families in utter grief, is unforget-
table—as memorable as the grieving of the Egyptians for their only
children, their lost firstborn.

12. Gen. 9:6; 37:22; Num. 35:33; Deut. 21:7; 1 Sam. 25:31; 2 Kings 21:16; Isa. 59:7.

6

Spirit Filling

Before reading this chapter, explore these texts:

>> Genesis 41:25–45

>> Exodus 28:1–5

>> Exodus 31:1–11; 36:1–7

>> Daniel 4:1–18

>> Daniel 5:1–16

>> Daniel 6:1–5

>> Micah 3:5–8

W hen the day of Pentecost had come, they were all together in one place. And suddenly from heaven there came a sound like the rush of a violent wind, and it filled the entire house where they were sitting. Divided tongues, as of fire, appeared among them, and a tongue rested on each of them. All of them were filled with the Holy Spirit and began to speak in other languages, as the Spirit gave them ability" (Acts 2:1–4). The contours of filling with the spirit here, at the birth of the church, are clear. Having waited expectantly for weeks on end, the followers of Jesus, finally filled with the holy spirit, experienced tongues as of fire and proclaimed God's praiseworthy acts in foreign languages. Fundamental to this portrait of inspiration is the belief that Jesus's followers received what they lacked before—not just the fullness of the spirit but the holy spirit, period.

Filling with the spirit in Israel's Scriptures looks, at first blush, like a similar experience. The prophet Micah claims to be filled with the spirit. The artisans who construct the tabernacle are filled with the spirit of wisdom. Joseph and Daniel are said to have the spirit within them. Each of these, it seems, receives the spirit to do something remarkable, whether to interpret dreams or strange handwriting on a wall or to prophesy or to build a tent for God in the wilderness. For this, they need to receive the spirit.

Or so it seems. Similarities between the Old and New Testaments are seductive, making it tempting to read the Old in light of the New. But that would be a grave mistake, since there are ample clues in Israel's Scriptures to indicate that being filled with the spirit in those texts is not quite the same as it is in the letters and stories of the early church. If we carefully attend to those clues rather than quickly making the Old Testament mirror the New, we will encounter untold insight into the spirit that complements the New Testament.

Joseph

From the story of Joseph (perhaps one of the oldest stories in the Jewish Bible) to the story of Daniel (one of the latest, which can be dated to the second century BCE), various Israelite and Jewish authors expressed their belief that human beings could be filled with a spirit from God. This, one of the most enduring refrains related to the spirit in the Jewish Scriptures, also offers something fresh: not so much the advent of the spirit from without as the stirring of the spirit-breath within.

In a haunting tale, Pharaoh, ruler of Egypt, has a disturbing dream that none of his advisers can interpret. Pharaoh's chief cupbearer, whose dream Joseph had interpreted while both were prisoners, recalls Joseph's unparalleled skills in dream interpretation. So Joseph is wrested from prison and taken to Pharaoh, whose dream he readily interprets. Pharaoh in response asks the question, "Can we find anyone else like this—one in whom is the spirit of God?" (Gen. 41:38). He then provides a nimble answer to his own question: "Since God has shown you all this, there is no one discerning and wise [like] you" (41:39). The parallel is striking. Pharaoh asks if anyone can be found "*like this*—one in whom is (the) spirit of God" and answers that "there is no one discerning and wise *like you*." Even an Egyptian—an outsider—can see the connection between the spirit of God within Joseph and Joseph's extraordinary wisdom.

The process by which Joseph has become a man of the spirit is not apparent on the surface of the story, but it is apparent nonetheless. The exceptional quality of *rûaḥ 'ĕlōhîm* in Joseph is the product of lifelong discipline rather than a sudden influx of the spirit that gifts him with extraordinary abilities.

When Pharaoh attributes Joseph's ability to interpret dreams to the divine character of *rûaḥ within* him, he does not describe the divine spirit that has come upon Joseph or rests upon him. The implication is that the spirit within Joseph has been his from birth. This understanding is borne out by earlier references to the spirit in the book of Genesis. Genesis 6:3, for instance, reads, "My *rûaḥ* shall not abide in mortals forever, for they are flesh, their days shall be one hundred twenty years." At issue in Genesis 6:3 is the length of an entire life span. The scenario is similar in the flood story, in which God destroys nearly all of those who have the "*rûaḥ* of life" (6:17; 7:15) or "the breath of the *rûaḥ* of life" (7:22, my translation). Spirit—*rûaḥ*—in the biblical book of Genesis is the spirit-breath that can be found not only within all people but within all animals as well.

Yet not all humans and animals have the same *quality* of spirit as Joseph—a quality that prompts the pharaoh to identify this *rûaḥ* as spirit *of God*. Joseph honed his skills at dream interpretation from his youth. He interpreted—to his brothers' chagrin—dreams in which sheaves and stars bowed down to one person in particular: Joseph (Gen. 37:5–11). In Egyptian prison, he interpreted the dreams of the cupbearer and the baker (Gen. 40). The step to Pharaoh's dream was a small one in light of Joseph's lifelong experience at dream interpretation. His astonishing ability to interpret dreams was not a new capacity fueled by an influx of the spirit—what might be called a charismatic endowment—but the result of a lifetime of learning, a protracted period of practice.

Another clue to the significance of the spirit within Joseph is that he does more than interpret dreams. He also appends to the interpretation of Pharaoh's dream pointed instruction that goes well beyond dream interpretation: Pharaoh should set aside a fifth of the grain during the good years, et cetera (Gen. 41:33–37). This too is evidence of the spirit of God in Joseph—precisely at this point in the story Pharaoh recognizes the spirit of God in Joseph—and this too is the product of hard-won experience. In the course of his life in Egypt, Joseph had been in charge of the house of Potiphar, who was captain of the palace guard, and of the prison to which Potiphar consigned him. He served so well over both Potiphar's house and the prison that neither Potiphar nor the chief jailer had to pay the least attention to what lay under Joseph's care (Gen. 39:6, 23). By the time Pharaoh identifies Joseph as one in whom is *rûaḥ* of God, then, Joseph is well practiced in both dream interpretation and administration.

This triad of the spirit of God within, practice in dream interpretation, and the exercise of administrative foresight composes the essential ingredients of Joseph's inspiration. His is a life lived well, with skills well learned and wisdom gotten hold of throughout a lifetime of pain and disappointment. These are the characteristics that prompt Pharaoh to ask, "Can we find anyone else like this—one in whom is (the) spirit of God?" (Gen. 41:38) and then to answer his own question: "Since God is making known all of this to you, there is no one discerning and wise like you" (41:39). When, therefore, Pharaoh detects an association between the presence of the spirit in Joseph and Joseph's remarkable wisdom, he draws the first indisputable connection between the spirit-breath and lifelong learning—what might be called *inspired learning*—in the Old Testament.

Micah

If the story of Joseph furnishes one of the earliest prose instances of the association of the spirit and wisdom in the Jewish Scriptures, the book of Micah, written as early as the eighth century BCE, supplies the earliest prophetic oracle. Micah rejected the sort of urban politics that preoccupied Isaiah, his contemporary. He eschewed the sort of vaunted—Micah might have called it florid and pretentious—call-vision that Isaiah experienced as a devotee of the Jerusalem temple (Isa. 6), when Isaiah found himself with a ringside seat at the holy of holies, where he saw God robed and surrounded by fiery seraphim. More to the point, Micah railed against all revelations and visions of his prophetic opponents. He excoriated other prophets—*false* prophets, to Micah's mind—for prophesying for profit and forecasted that they would be "without vision" and "without revelation." These "seers" and "diviners," who discerned direction in various signs, such as wisps of sacrificial smoke, would have nothing to say because they said little more than what the royal family wanted to hear. Micah's message is unequivocal:

> Thus says the LORD concerning the prophets
>> who lead my people astray,
> who cry "Peace"
>> when they have something to eat,
> but declare war against those
>> who put nothing into their mouths.
> Therefore it shall be night to you, without vision,
>> and darkness to you, without revelation.
> The sun shall go down upon the prophets,
>> and the day shall be black over them;
> the seers shall be disgraced,
>> and the diviners put to shame;
> they shall all cover their lips,
>> for there is no answer from God. (Mic. 3:5–7)

For all he excoriates and eschews, Micah does not snub the spirit of God. "But as for me," claims Micah,

> I am filled with power,
>> with the spirit of the LORD,
>> and with justice and might,
> to declare to Jacob his transgression
>> and to Israel his sin. (Mic. 3:8)

As in the oracles of the book of Isaiah, the spirit is joined at the hip to justice as well as to power and capability. Yet this is not the whole picture. Micah's claim to being "filled with power, with (the) spirit of the LORD, and with justice and might" is not a claim to a fresh endowment with the spirit, an influx of power or knowledge. Micah's claim is to the *rûaḥ* understood as a permanent endowment within that inspires him continually to live justly and to speak powerfully.

The linchpin of this realization is that Micah is filled with three permanent qualities: strength, justice, and might. These qualities are not temporary endowments. Justice, for example, is so essential that Micah begins his cross-examination of the leaders with the rhetorical question, "Should you not know justice?" (Mic. 3:1). Of course they should! Justice is so axiomatic, in fact, that Micah can indict his people for failing to know what anyone should know: "He [God] has told you, O mortal, what is good; and what does the LORD require of you but to do justice, and to love kindness, and to walk humbly with your God?" (6:8). The justice with which Micah is filled, like the spirit with which he is filled, is a permanent part of his character, not a transitory or late-on-the-scene endowment that prompts him on occasion to preach with integrity. *Everyone* should know what justice is. Micah certainly does. He is not filled with justice conveniently or occasionally, nor is he filled with the spirit sporadically or expediently. Justice is not, therefore, the product of a peculiar prophetic revelation. People know justice already, or ought to: "God has told you, O mortal, what is good."

The nature of the spirit that fills Micah is apparent as well in his indictment of other prophets. False prophets look for inspiration in visions, revelations, and divinations—short-lived modes of divine disclosure. Micah's message to Judah, in contrast, arises from his *always* being filled with power, justice, the Lord's spirit, and might. Other prophets' transitory revelations and visions will turn to night (Mic. 3:6); Micah, in contrast, is filled with qualities that can never be taken away.

Micah allows for little common ground between himself and false prophets. They support the status quo while he exposes sins. They preach false peace while he recognizes future perils. And perhaps most essential of all, they feed on visions and revelations while he is filled with strength, *rûaḥ* of the Lord, justice, and might.

Micah's claim to the spirit reverberates with his contemporary, Isaiah of Jerusalem (Isa. 1–39). Although Micah was rural and Isaiah urban, although Micah criticized Jerusalem and Isaiah operated comfortably in its corridors of power, both prophets affirm the relationship between the spirit and justice. Neither connects the spirit to revelations. Neither sees the spirit as the source of a temporary experience. Both connect the spirit to what is sustained, knowable, and just—in short, to what is *learned*. The inspired ruler that Isaiah imagines and the inspired prophet Micah share a penchant for justice accomplished through keen words. Isaiah's anointed ruler

> shall not judge by what his eyes see,
>   or decide by what his ears hear;
> but with *justice* he shall judge the poor,
>   and decide with equity for the meek of the earth;
> he shall strike the earth with the rod of his mouth,
>   and with the breath of his lips he shall kill the wicked.
> *Justice* shall be the belt around his waist,
>   and faithfulness the belt around his loins. (Isa. 11:3–5,
>   italics added)

Isaiah's description of the inspired ruler mirrors the elements of Micah's call:

> I am filled with power,
>   with the spirit of the LORD,
>   and with *justice* and might,
> to declare to Jacob his transgression
>   and to Israel his sin. (Mic. 3:8, italics added)

This passage from Isaiah fits perfectly with Micah; Micah's autobiographical description fits perfectly with Isaiah's anointed ruler. The ruler on whom the spirit rests is known especially for justice (Isa. 11:3–5); Micah, filled with the spirit, is known for his relentless commitment to justice (Mic. 3:5–8). In both Isaiah's description of the inspired ruler and Micah's description of his own conviction, the ingredients of knowledge, honest words, justice, and spirit combine to create a surprisingly unified point of intersection between an elite urban prophet and a rural critic of the Jerusalem elite. Both express the belief that *rûaḥ* is a permanent presence characterized by knowledge hard won and justice made concrete.

What we do not know about Isaiah's inspired ruler and Micah, the inspired prophet, is when the spirit would become their permanent endowment. For the ruler, inspiration seems to come with an appointment or anointing as messiah or king. For Micah, the onset of inspiration is less clear; it may begin either at birth or some sort of calling. Micah's words are too brief to clarify this. What we do know is that, as early as the late eighth century (the 700s BCE), two prophets drew a tight connection between the spirit as a permanent endowment and a life committed to justice—to justice learned, to justice taught. At this early phase in Israel's history, two independent voices communicated with utter clarity that inspiration and learning, rather than revelations and visions, are the essential pair lying at the base of courageous prophecy and an inspired reign.

Artisans in the Desert

More than a small swath of Israel's history is devoted to meticulous instructions about how a wilderness tent, the tabernacle, should be prepared (Exod. 25:1–31:11; 35:4–33). Though these instructions may be overshadowed by the Ten Words (20:1–17) or even the Covenant Code, arguably the earliest laws in the Hebrew Scriptures (20:22–23:19), these instructions for the tabernacle are not only more extensive than both of those put together but even purport to be the product of direct divine revelation at Mount Sinai, just as much as the Ten Commandments.

The story of the tabernacle's construction offers examples of unsurpassed generosity.[1] Although this characteristic of the story may be overshadowed by an apparently dreary inventory of provisions

---

1. Most scholars regard the bulk of this story as a postexilic or Persian-era (after 539 BCE) composition because its interest in the details of worship and worship places is comparable to 1–2 Chronicles.

and physical dimensions, this love for detail drives home the impulse of Israelite generosity. All of what was made, constructed, woven, sewn, stitched, dyed, hammered, and overlaid came from the freewill offering of those whose hearts prompted them. This was a moment of sumptuous giving, and it is no surprise that the lavish language of filling with the spirit should occur here.

Inspired Artisans

When it comes time to sew vestments for Aaron and the priesthood, God tells Moses, "And you shall speak to all the wise of heart whom I have filled with a spirit of wisdom, and they will make Aaron's vestments" (Exod. 28:3, my translation). The association of the spirit with learning—God fills *artisans* with a spirit of wisdom—is incontestable in this bit of instruction. Yet something more is discernible: God selects these skilled laborers not so that they may receive an endowment of a spirit of wisdom but because *already* they have demonstrated their skill. The skilled, the wise of heart, are to be filled with the spirit of wisdom.[2]

The realization that the artisans are *already* wise of heart raises the question of how God fills the artisans with a spirit of wisdom if they are already filled with wisdom. This is a conundrum, however, only if the verb *fill* refers to the first-time filling of an empty vessel—it does not.

The word *fill* (*millēʾ*) can describe an initial filling: a skin is filled with water (Gen. 21:19), a bag with grain (42:25), a horn with oil (1 Sam. 16:1). This is by no means the whole of its meaning. Yet the verb moves readily from initial filling to completion to filling full to fulfillment. A pregnancy comes to term—*is filled* (Gen. 25:24). A period of purification is completed—*filled* (Lev. 12:4, 6).[3] Spaces, too, are filled. When Egyptian houses are filled with swarms of flies, more than a few flies can be expected (Exod. 8:21; MT 8:17). When

---

2. Throughout this story (e.g., Exod. 36:8), the phrase *wise of heart* refers to skilled laborers in contrast to unskilled. For a more detailed analysis, see my *Filled with the Spirit* (Grand Rapids: Eerdmans, 2009), 51–65.

3. Jacob's wait for Rachel was over—*filled* (Gen. 29:21). A vow is *fulfilled* (Num. 6:5). Banquets end—*are filled* (Esther 1:5). The Babylonian exile ends—*is filled* (Jer. 25:12).

the hem of God's robe fills the temple, more than a tip of the garment occupies the inner sanctum (Isa. 6:1). When Jeremiah protests that the land is filled with idols, he refers to more than a few idols (Jer. 16:18). When the Jordan fills its banks, the river floods those banks (Josh. 3:15).[4]

From this perspective, the simple phrase "whom I have filled with a spirit of wisdom" suggests full-filling—fruition, wholeness, skill fully honed. This simple verb *fill* communicates that there is now more than enough spirit within these gifted laborers to complete the task at hand exquisitely. The artisans are not moderately well equipped. They are full to the brim with a wise spirit. Their hearts, in short, are full of wisdom, flooded with the skills they have cultivated, which will allow them to construct a tent for God's presence in the wilderness. In an extravagant scene, in which the hues and textures of the priestly garments are vivid, the artisans who produce such glorious garments are depicted in equally lavish terms as "the wise of heart whom I filled with a spirit of wisdom."[5]

Chief Architects and Artisans

The artisans' leaders are especially full of the spirit. Of Bezalel and Oholiab, God says to Moses,

See, I have called by name Bezalel son of Uri son of Hur, of the tribe of Judah: and I have filled him with (the)[6] spirit of God, with wisdom, intelligence, and knowledge in every kind of craft, to devise artistic designs, to work in gold, silver, and bronze, in cutting stones for setting, and in carving wood, in every kind of craft. Moreover, I have appointed with him Oholiab son of Ahisamach, of the tribe of Dan; and I have given wisdom in the heart of all the wise of heart, so that they may make all that I have commanded you. (Exod. 31:2–6 alt.)

4. Similar understandings of filling occur in 1 Kings 8:10, 15; 2 Chron. 6:4; Jer. 23:24; 44:25; Ezek. 40:34–35; 44:4; Hab. 2:14.
5. For slightly more analysis, including a brief discussion of the adjective *full* and the noun *fullness*, see my *Filled with the Spirit*, 52–58.
6. In this and the next few quotations, the Hebrew *wā'ămallē' 'ōṯô rûaḥ 'ĕlōhîm* could be translated in a variety of ways: "filled him with the spirit of God," "filled him with a spirit of God," "filled him with spirit of God." NRSV translates, "filled him with divine spirit."

Bezalel and his capable sidekick resurface when Moses says,

> See, the LORD has called by name Bezalel son of Uri son of Hur, of the tribe of Judah; he has filled him with (the) spirit of God, with wisdom, intelligence, and knowledge in every kind of craft, to devise artistic designs, to work in gold, silver, and bronze, in cutting stones for setting, and in carving wood, in every kind of craft. And he put into his heart to teach, both him and Oholiab son of Ahisamach, of the tribe of Dan. He has filled them with wisdom of heart to do every kind of work done by an artisan or by a designer or by an embroiderer in blue, purple, and crimson yarns, and in fine linen, or by a weaver—by any sort of artisan or skilled designer. (Exod. 35:30–35 alt.)

In these parallel depictions, the correspondence between spirit and heart, which described the artisans in Exodus 28:3 (the *wise of heart*, whom I *have filled with [the] spirit of wisdom*), occurs with utter precision. A similar parallel occurs in Exodus 35:30–35:

> 35:31: [God] *has filled him* [Bezalel] *with (the) spirit of God, with wisdom . . . for every craft.*
>
> 35:35: [God] *filled them* [Bezalel and Oholiab] *with wisdom of heart . . . to do every craft.*

Alongside the corresponding language of "wisdom of heart," God's filling with "spirit of God, with wisdom" solidifies the relationship between the spirit and learning; these are skilled artisans who will now construct the tabernacle. They are selected because of their skill. Yet there is, as in Micah's oracle, something more here. This text, like Micah's claim, does not communicate a fresh influx of the spirit. It suggests something permanent, enduring. The heart is not something that comes and goes. Nor is the spirit. The mirror images of heart and spirit suggest rather that filling with *rûaḥ* ought to be understood as a filling *full* of a spirit that the artisans and their leaders have cultivated through a lifetime of learning.

Like the other artisans, Bezalel and Oholiab's hearts were already skilled, their spirits already knowledgeable, in which case this gift of wisdom came to hearts and spirits that were already wise through acquired learning. Although there is no new heart or spirit in this narrative, there is something new here: at this unique moment in Israel's history, the spirit of God, with which God had filled Bezalel and the artisans from the start, was made even fuller with wisdom, insight, and intelligence. These artisans and their capable leaders were full to the brim with God's spirit, overflowing with *rûaḥ*, in tandem with a lifetime of learning. They were consequently capable of constructing a sacred tent in a godforsaken wilderness.

Inspired Teachers

It is essential not to let all the talk of inspiration in these stories obscure the centrality of learning. What Bezalel and Oholiab did with their own inspired learning is telling: "And [God] gave in his heart to teach, both him and Oholiab son of Ahisamach, of the tribe of Dan" (Exod. 35:34, my translation).[7] Simply put, they *taught* the artisans.

This discreet line suggests a good deal about how the artisans came to be "filled with (a) spirit of wisdom," how God could claim, "I have given wisdom in the heart of all the wise of heart." While the image of filling with the spirit may suggest direct, divine intervention—a charismatic endowment—the role of teaching suggests otherwise. The artisans were filled with a spirit of wisdom and given wisdom in their heart because they learned from extraordinary teachers who had mastered every craft.

Daniel

The latest stories of Israelites filled with the spirit are a mirror of the earliest; Daniel looks much like Joseph. The stories of Daniel are probably the product of the Maccabean era (ca. 167–160 BCE), though the stories are set in an earlier, horrific era at the onset of the Babylonian exile.

---

7. The translation of the NRSV, with the verb *inspire*, is too evocative of a charismatic endowment: "And he has inspired him to teach, both him and Oholiab son of Ahisamach, of the tribe of Dan." It is better to translate the Hebrew verb *give* simply as "gave," following the lead of the Greek translation, the Septuagint: "God *gave* into his heart to teach."

In the stories that coalesce around Daniel, four men are among those taken by force to exile in Babylon sometime after Jerusalem was crushed in 587 BCE. Babylon includes Daniel and these men among those who are to be trained to lead the Israelites in exile (Dan. 1:1). For the next several chapters, Daniel does amazing things: he interprets Nebuchadnezzar's dream of a huge statue (Dan. 2); he and his companions are rescued from a fiery furnace (Dan. 3), into which they were thrown for failing to worship Nebuchadnezzar's golden statue (Dan. 2); he interprets Nebuchadnezzar's dream about a huge tree cut down in its prime (Dan. 4); he interprets the handwriting that appears on a wall during a party thrown by Belshazzar, Nebuchadnezzar's son (Dan. 5); and finally, he is rescued from a lion's den (Dan. 6), into which he was thrown because of the jealousy of King Darius's political cronies.

The presence of *rûaḥ* in these stories lasts for three generations—a substantial bit of time. Daniel is not just a young man in a lion's den; he is a man who is inevitably identified with the spirit while he grows old.

During the first generation, after Daniel interprets his dream, King Nebuchadnezzar of Babylon claims three times that Daniel has "a spirit of a/the holy God(s) in him" (Dan. 4:8, 9, 18; MT 4:5, 6, 15; my translation). The Aramaic is more ambiguous than most English translations. This could be translated in a variety of ways, including "the spirit of the holy God in him" or "a spirit of holy gods in him." Whatever the translation, the presence of a holy spirit in Daniel is central to this text.

During the second generation, Nebuchadnezzar's daughter-in-law, after hearing about the baffling writing that appears on a wall during Belshazzar's party, mirrors her father's language: "There is a man in your kingdom who is endowed with a spirit of the holy gods. In the days of your father he was found to have enlightenment, understanding, and wisdom like the wisdom of the gods." She recalls that "an excellent spirit, knowledge, and understanding to interpret dreams, explain riddles, and solve problems were found in this Daniel" (Dan. 5:11–12). Her husband, Nebuchadnezzar's son Belshazzar, also knows about Daniel's *spirit of God* (*rûaḥ ʾĕlāhîn*) and *excellent wisdom* (5:14).

During the third generation, Darius of Media plans to appoint Daniel to the heights of imperial policy because "an excellent spirit is in him" (Dan. 6:3; MT 6:4). This is a reiteration of what was said during the prior generation.

This is ample spirit language, and it fits the pattern of the stories of Joseph, of the artisans who engineered the tabernacle, and of Micah's claim to the spirit. Throughout three generations—Nebuchadnezzar, Belshazzar, and Darius—Daniel exhibits such wisdom that a succession of foreign rulers recognizes a *rûaḥ* in him that could have come only from God. If Daniel possesses wisdom throughout three generations, it is not because he occasionally receives a special endowment of the spirit of God but because the spirit within him is the perennial source of enlightenment, wisdom, and prescience.

In over half a dozen references to the spirit in close sequence, in fact, the spirit is allied with Daniel's wisdom. In the second story, an especially conspicuous verbal correspondence between the spirit and wisdom rises to the surface:

"*rûaḥ yattîrâ* . . . in him"—intense *spirit* in him (5:12);

"*ḥokmâ yattîrâ* . . . in him"—intense *wisdom* in him (5:14).

This correspondence raises the question of the source of Daniel's wisdom. It is possible that this wisdom is some sort of temporary charismatic gift, though this interpretation falters on a couple of fronts. The first is that Daniel, like Joseph, on whom the figure of Daniel is modeled, gained this wisdom principally through discipline. In the opening story of the book of Daniel, Babylon trained elite Israelites who were "without physical defect and handsome, versed in every branch of wisdom, endowed with knowledge and insight, and competent to serve in the king's palace; they were to be taught the literature and language of the Chaldeans" (1:4). As the story unfolds, Daniel and three of his closest friends used none of their brains or brawn to get ahead in the sphere of imperial power. Unlike nearly all of the other royal refugees, who for three years were treated to lavish food and wine from the king's own table to prepare them for a lifetime in the king's court, Daniel "resolved that he would not defile himself with the royal rations of food and wine; so he asked the palace master to allow him not to defile himself" (1:8). Together Daniel and his three companions ate vegetables rather than rich food and wine. During this period of self-imposed austerity, "God gave knowledge and skill in every aspect of literature and wisdom; Daniel also had insight into all visions and dreams" (1:17). It is here, in the crucible of Daniel's resistance to royal rations, in his repudiation of ambition, in his rejection of power, in his penchant for simplicity, in his refusal to seek status, that Daniel is first recognized as an interpreter of visions and dreams. At the end of this period, "in every matter of wisdom and understanding concerning which the king inquired of them, he found them ten times better than all the magicians and enchanters in his whole kingdom" (1:20).

These descriptions, of course, could be interpreted to mean that God gave Daniel and his companions knowledge, wisdom, and understanding as temporary gifts, as occasional or even recurrent outbursts of the spirit—except for the earlier detail that this entire group of young men who were taken into exile were "young men without physical defect and handsome, versed in every branch of wisdom, endowed with knowledge and insight, and competent to serve in the king's palace; they were to be taught the literature and language of the Chaldeans" (Dan. 1:4). In short, Daniel and his companions were already well educated by the time they resisted royal rations. Inspiration in this story is the product of a rich symbiosis among human fidelity, learning, and the gift of divine wisdom. Through this rejection of human comfort combined with intense education, Daniel came first to interpret dreams—a skill that would later in life be attributed by a bevy of foreign rulers to the *rûaḥ* in him.

Something else to note is that the spirit and wisdom within Daniel are described as *yattîrâ rûaḥ* (or *rûaḥ yattîrā᾽*) (5:14; 6:3). The translation of *yattîrâ* as "excellent," such as in the NRSV, is deceptive. The Aramaic and Hebrew communicate something else: extreme degree. The brilliance of Nebuchadnezzar's statue was *extreme* (2:31). The fiery furnace into which Shadrach, Meshach, and Abednego were cast was *extremely* hot (3:22). A beast in Daniel's visions was *extremely* terrifying (7:19). This word communicates something other than excellence. It communicates sheer brilliance, sheer heat, sheer terror, and *sheer spirit*—spirit so perfectly spirit that it is clearly a spirit from God. This is what Daniel possessed. This is what distinguished Daniel.[8]

Spirit as the Font of Skill

The belief that God fills human beings with a spirit that can be cultivated into a reservoir of skill and wisdom lasted from Israel's earliest stories to its latest. Establishing a chronology of Israel's literature is notoriously challenging, but this much may be said: If the story of Joseph can be dated to the period before the fall of the Northern Kingdom in 722 BCE, if the call of Micah is from about the time of that fall, if the story of the tabernacle is dated to the Persian era (after 539 BCE), and if the book of Daniel has a Maccabean origin (167–160 BCE), then it is possible to trace a line of interpretation spanning at least six hundred years. The baseline of this belief was the conviction that the spirit does not come and go. God-given, the spirit exists within human beings, among whom some hone their skills so exceptionally that they are characterized by a *rûaḥ* full of wisdom.

Though in a different idiom, the portrait of Daniel—filled with sheer spirit, sheer wisdom for a full three generations—shares a core conviction with the stories of Joseph, the artisans who engineered the tabernacle, and even the prophet Micah. This conviction has to do with an understanding of the spirit as a lifelong reservoir of wisdom and skill.

In the stories of Joseph and Daniel, arguably among the earliest and latest in the Jewish Scriptures, both men interpret the inscrutable and ably administrate great empires because they labored earlier in their lives to learn—Joseph in prison and Potiphar's house, Daniel in early exile. If Joseph and Daniel possess extraordinary knowledge, it is not because they occasionally receive a charismatic endowment of the spirit but because the spirit within them is the perpetual source of enlightenment, wisdom, and prescience. This wisdom is the product of a mysterious association of inspiration and education; both are essential to what distinguishes these men, whose early labors come to fruition in the presence of foreign rulers, who recognize that the

8. In *Fresh Air: The Holy Spirit for an Inspired Life* (Brewster, MA: Paraclete, 2012), 42–67, I devote an entire chapter to the story of Daniel in a popular style.

source of their wisdom is the spirit within them. This spirit, not a come-lately spirit but a spirit from birth, is recognizable, in Daniel's case at least, for three generations.

Daniel's knowledge is reminiscent, too, of the story of the desert artisans who were filled with *rûaḥ*—spirit of wisdom—because they had honed their skill under the capable direction of Bezalel and Oholiab, their inspired teachers, who themselves were filled "with (the) spirit of God, with wisdom, intelligence, and knowledge in every kind of craft."

Daniel's wisdom mirrors Micah's as well; Micah claimed to be filled, unlike other prophets whose revelation came by fits and starts, with God's spirit, along with power, might, and justice. Justice, Micah knows, is learned; it requires no special endowment.

For Joseph, the artisans, Daniel, and possibly Micah too, the spirit is a lifelong presence within, a perennial source of wisdom. This conception of inspiration is probably different from Isaiah's inspired messiah, upon whom the spirit comes to rest, but the association of the spirit with knowledge, wisdom, and justice is no different at all. A single, seamless association lies at the base of these two quite different modes of the spirit's presence.

The scenario in the story of Daniel is also different from the book of Chronicles, where the spirit comes upon key figures who speak to Israel and its leaders. Men like Azariah (2 Chron. 15:1) and Jahaziel (2 Chron. 20:14) presumably receive the spirit temporarily, yet what they say reflects a lifetime of learning, as they take up ancient traditions for new ends. The spirit, in short, inspires them to speak from a surfeit of learning; there is an undeniable connection between learning and inspiration in what they have to say. While their experience of the spirit may be temporary rather than lifelong, occasional rather than perennial, with respect to the link between spirit and learning, the men of Chronicles, like Isaiah's inspired ruler, are no different from Daniel or Joseph or Micah or the artisans and their talented teachers. For all of them, there is no gulf, no chasm at all, between life in the spirit and a lifetime of learning. Education and inspiration reinforce one another.[9]

9. To discover a more detailed exploration of the biblical texts in this chapter, consult the detailed analysis in my *Filled with the Spirit*, 34–105.

7

Spirit Cleansing

Before reading this chapter, explore these texts:

>> Psalm 51
>> Ezekiel 11:14–25
>> Ezekiel 18:1–32
>> Ezekiel 36:16–32

During the second century BCE, the Greco-Roman universe swirled in Palestine as Jews wrestled naked with their Gentile counterparts in the gymnasium, as the genius of the Greek educational system drew Jews into its orbit, and as building after building that looked more at home in Athens or Rome than Jerusalem filled the skyline of Palestinian coastal cities and urban centers. The Jewish people of Qumran would have none of it. They chose to react to the allure of Greek culture by sequestering themselves along the shores of the Dead Sea in a little patch of barren land that measures barely more than a football field. These people could not be lured away by the bright lights of Greek festivals and games, by gymnasia and lavish theaters, nor were they enticed elsewhere by the amenities of Roman engineering and architecture, not even the cool, fresh, drinkable water that flowed through their aqueducts.

Even when an earthquake devastated their outpost in 31 BCE, they chose to stay put and rebuild rather than relocate to a more alluring and comfortable site.

Purity was of the essence for this small community that bequeathed to the world the enduring legacy of the Dead Sea Scrolls. They would have nothing to do with the Syrians, Greeks, or Romans and even less to do, it seems, with Jews who followed a lunar calendar rather than their solar one, who spent their lives doing business with Gentiles, and who worshiped at a temple that the people of Qumran believed was hopelessly corrupt.

Given its strictures and constraints, an individual could enter the community at Qumran only through a stringent, several-year process. At the end of this protracted process, a man (probably only men) could be initiated into the community. This was not a matter of merely joining; it was a matter of *purification*. A lengthy description of their initiation ritual draws a rigid line between outsiders and insiders, the impure and the pure, the unrepentant and the faithful. The "knowledge, strength and wealth" of the unrepentant "are not to enter the society of the *Yaḥad*.[1] Surely, he plows in the muck of wickedness, so defiling stains would mar his repentance. Yet he cannot be justified by what his willful heart declares lawful, preferring to gaze on darkness rather than the ways of light. With such an eye he cannot be reckoned faultless."[2] So unfaithful is he that "ceremonies of atonement cannot restore his innocence, neither cultic waters his purity. He cannot be sanctified by baptism in oceans and rivers, nor purified by mere ritual bathing. Unclean, unclean shall he be all the days that he rejects the laws of God, refusing to be disciplined in the *Yaḥad* of His society."[3] External rituals, in short, cannot solve the dilemma of hard-heartedness or dissolve the grip of sin.

The solution to sin, this small band of Jewish believers understood, lies in the presence of the spirit, which is to be found, according

1. *Yaḥad* is a transliteration of a Hebrew word that refers to the "community" at Qumran. Translations of the Dead Sea Scrolls are from Martin Abegg, Michael Wise, and Edward Cook, *The Dead Sea Scrolls: A New English Translation*, rev. ed. (New York: HarperCollins, 2005).

2. *Community Rule* (1QS) 3.2–4.

3. *Community Rule* (1QS) 3.4–6.

to their writings, exclusively in the community at Qumran: "For only through the spirit pervading God's true society can there be atonement for a man's ways, all of his iniquities; thus only can he gaze upon the light of life and so be joined to His truth by His holy spirit, purified from all iniquity. Through an upright and humble attitude his sin may be covered, and by humbling himself before all God's laws his flesh can be made clean. Only thus can he really receive the purifying waters and be purged by the cleansing flow."[4]

The connection between internal purification by the holy spirit and external purification by water may seem to Christians like it belongs in the New Testament, especially in descriptions of baptism.[5] It certainly would be at home there, given that the New Testament is a thoroughly Jewish collection of documents. The community at Qumran predated the early church, anticipating many of its characteristics by a century or more, though with one salient distinction. The community at Qumran embraced an intensity of isolation that shunned Gentiles; the early church, in contrast, expended enormous energy to reach the Gentile world.

This association of the spirit with purity also made its way into various retellings of the Jewish Scriptures, such as the book of *Jubilees*, a fascinating early Jewish revision of the biblical book of Genesis, which, if the number of copies they possessed is any indication, the community at Qumran prized. At the start of *Jubilees*, Moses finds himself with God on Mount Sinai, where he intercedes for his fellow Israelites who wait below: "O Lord, let your mercy be lifted up upon your people, and create for them an upright spirit. . . . Create a pure heart and a holy spirit for them. And do not let them be ensnared by their sin henceforth and forever" (*Jub.* 1:19–20). Moses's plea here is an amalgamation of Psalm 51, with its reference to an "upright spirit," and Ezekiel 36:25–26, with its association of a clean heart with a new spirit. God responds (*Jub.* 1:22–25) in kind with a promise shaped by Psalm 51 and Ezekiel 11:19–20: "And I shall cut off the foreskin of their heart and the foreskin of the heart of their descendants. And I shall create for them a holy spirit, and I shall

4. *Community Rule* (1QS) 3.6–9.
5. E.g., Acts 2:38; Titus 3:4–7; Heb. 10:21–22.

purify them so that they will not turn away from following me from that day and forever. And their souls will cleave to me and to all my commandments."[6]

This insistence upon purity—purification—through the holy spirit is both intense and institutionalized in the community at Qumran. It is not a matter of sense or sensibility; it is part of their initiation ceremony as well as their quotidian experience, which demanded a daily enforcement of regulations to ensure purity. This penchant for purity even permeated their understanding of Scripture, mediated as it was through stories they cherished, such as the book of *Jubilees*.

No such systematic connection between the spirit and purification characterizes the Hebrew Bible. Still, as the book of *Jubilees* suggests, the association was there, however infrequent or inchoate it may have been, in poems such as Psalm 51 and the prophetic book of Ezekiel.

A Renewed Heart and Spirit

At some point in Israel's history, a poet composed a poignant recollection of David's illicit tryst with Bathsheba—whether inadvertently or intentionally we do not know. As in so many other stories, oracles, and poems, *rûaḥ* in Psalm 51 is not merely breath. Nor is it the divine spirit understood as a temporary endowment. Nor is it a gift that assures salvation. This spirit is, rather, an alchemy of spirit-breath that is so much more expressive of Hebrew *rûaḥ* than any single English word, whether *wind*, *breath*, *spirit*, or *Spirit*. Too much is at stake in this poem—revulsion in the face of sin and dread in the face of death—to reduce *rûaḥ*, a word that occurs four times in this single psalm, to any one of these meager meanings.

The poet begs,

> Have mercy on me, O God,
> according to your steadfast love;
> according to your abundant mercy
> blot out my transgressions.

6. Translations of pseudepigraphical texts such as *Jubilees* are from James H. Charlesworth, ed., *The Old Testament Pseudepigrapha*, 2 vols. (New York: Doubleday, 1983, 1985).

Wash me thoroughly from my iniquity,
  and cleanse me from my sin.
For I know my transgressions,
  and my sin is ever before me.
Against you, you alone, have I sinned,
  and done what is evil in your sight,
so that you are justified in your sentence
  and blameless when you pass judgment.
Indeed, I was born guilty,
  a sinner when my mother conceived me. (Ps. 51:1–5; MT
    51:3–7)

Something has gone egregiously wrong in this lament, whether something as concrete as David's sexual dalliance with Bathsheba or some otherwise unknowable sin that every reader of the psalm can insert in private. The sense that something is dreadfully wrong could have led the poet to self-recrimination, to despair, to dejection even. It does not. This piercing realization of sin leads the poet not to self-denigration but to hope that lies beyond the cusp of his or her repulsive actions. The solution, the answer to the poet's plea, has *rûaḥ* written all over it:

Create in me a clean heart, O God,
  and renew a right *rûaḥ* within me.
Do not cast me away from your presence [*pānîm*],
  and do not take your holy *rûaḥ* from me.
Restore to me the joy of your salvation,
  and sustain in me a willing [ready] *rûaḥ*.
    (Ps. 51:10–12; MT 51:12–14)

This prayer for purification is not at all typical; the poet begins not with the language of public temple worship or private devotion but with the language of creation: "Create in me a clean heart, O God, and put a new and right spirit within me." The word *create* recalls vividly the second word in the Hebrew Bible: "In the beginning God *created* . . ." (Gen. 1:1). This command also resembles Ezekiel's valley of very many, very dry bones, a vision in which a new spirit within a shattered Israel replaces the old, where a new *adam* emerges from the valley of bleached bones, inspired by an amazing amalgamation of breath and the four winds—both are *rûaḥ* in Hebrew—rising slowly, noisily, and inevitably back to life (Ezek. 37:1–14).

The next line in the psalm, where the poet prays for God to make a *renewed* spirit within, underscores this heartfelt reality. Despite this cousin-like resemblance to the creation of the cosmos (Gen. 1) and the re-creation of Israel (Ezek. 37), Psalm 51 is concerned with a different arena of existence: not the deepest waters of the abyss but the depths of the human heart, not a nation rising from the dust with the influx of *rûaḥ* but the spirit-breath rhythmically pulsing within an individual's heart and lungs and veins and arteries—a world beyond the reach of human reparation.

This psalm suggests that hope does not rest entirely upon a new and altogether different heart. The psalm's first plea is for washing and cleansing rather than an entirely new creation. Despite the poet's conviction that he or she was conceived in sin, successive pleas point to the possibility of rehabilitation: the belief that God can teach the poet wisdom deep within (Ps. 51:6; MT 51:8); the conviction that cleansing and purging are still available (51:7; MT 51:9); and the assumption that physical healing is still possible, that crushed bones can again rejoice (51:8; MT 51:10). The poet is holding on for dear life; it is not entirely clear whether the poet is reminding God or himself that no sin is beyond the scope of God's penchant to create and re-create. Perhaps both, the poet knows, need reminding.

In light of these convictions, the urgent plea "Create in me a clean heart" is a prayer for cleansing, for transformation, for instruction in wisdom rather than for a miraculous transformation that does away with the old heart altogether. This is the gist of what the poet says later:

> For you have no delight in sacrifice;
> if I were to give a burnt offering, you would not be
> pleased.
> The sacrifice acceptable to God is a broken spirit;
> a broken and contrite heart, O God, you will not despise.
> (Ps. 51:16–17; MT 51:18–19)

There is still something that is acceptable to God: unadulterated contrition—a broken spirit, a broken heart. There remains, then, a measure of hope for forgiveness, for remediation, and for healing. There remains the possibility of a steadfast and generous spirit. If God will provide cleansing—a clean heart and a right spirit within— then God will not have to turn away God's face (*pānîm*) or take away God's holy spirit (*rûaḥ*) from the beleaguered poet.

The holy spirit that the poet fears God will take away is not the holy spirit God gives to people of faith, as in the Christian tradition. In this poem, the adjective *holy* is set readily beside other adjectives, such as *steadfast* and *ready*. These adjectives reveal that the spirit is a lifelong presence within the poet. The poet asks for a steadfast spirit, a generous spirit, a *holy* spirit, not for a limited period but for his entire life. In fact, the poet asks for a *restoration* of that spirit, along with a restoration of the joy of salvation, rather than a replacement of that spirit with a new one. The hope of this poem is that the poet's unholy spirit can be made holy again by God's cleansing.

Another clue to the understanding of *rûaḥ* in this poem lies in its indispensable relationship with the heart, which is also conceived as a permanent reality at the core of the poet's life. Together heart and spirit represent the essence of the poet, or what must be cleansed, instructed, and redirected. The relationship between these two core realities—heart and spirit—is evident in the taut parallels between a "clean heart" and "right spirit" (Ps. 51:12) and particularly between a "broken spirit" and "broken . . . heart" (51:19).

Heart and spirit could be so intimately related that they were considered one and the same—or nearly so. Deuteronomy 2:30, for example, recalls, "But King Sihon of Heshbon was not willing to let us pass through, for the LORD your God had hardened his spirit and made his heart defiant in order to hand him over to you, as he has now done." Israel's poets identify the brokenhearted with the crushed of spirit (Ps. 34:18; MT 34:19). They identify the faint of spirit with the appalled of heart (143:4). The prophet of Isaiah 56–66 joins pain of heart to anguish of spirit (Isa. 65:14).

The story of the artisans who constructed the tabernacle takes the intimate connection between spirit and heart to a new level: "And you shall speak to all the wise of heart, whom I have filled with a spirit of wisdom, that they make Aaron's vestments to consecrate him for my priesthood" (Exod. 28:3, my translation). Unfortunately, translators mask the Hebrew by translating the Hebrew words *spirit of wisdom* as "skill" (NRSV), "wisdom" (NIV), or "special abilities" (CEB). They also conceal the presence of the heart in the Hebrew phrase *wise of heart* with the translations "all who have ability" (NRSV), "skilled workers" (NIV), and "all who are skilled" (CEB). Once the clutter of translations is cleared, we can see clearly that the wise of heart are filled with a spirit of wisdom. In the Hebrew of this story, the relationship of spirit and heart communicates that both are permanent aspects of a human being, which God can prompt or fill to the brim.

The poet is not praying, therefore, about *the* holy spirit, which he or she received in an act of faith, a moment of inspiration, or a ritual such as baptism. The holy spirit is yoked to the steadfast heart. Both must be broken; both can be renewed.

The spirit, understood as a core dimension of the poet alongside the heart, brings clarity to the tandem request, "Do not cast me away from your presence [*pānîm*], and do not take your holy spirit [*rûaḥ*] from me" (Ps. 51:11). At its most fundamental level, casting from God's presence entails death. Jeremiah, after all, denounces false prophets and the Israelites who support them with the threat of annihilation: "I will . . . cast you away from my presence, you and the city that I gave to you and your ancestors. And I will bring upon you everlasting disgrace and perpetual shame, which shall not be forgotten" (Jer. 23:39–40). We can draw even closer to the poet's frantic plea by revisiting Psalm 104:29, where, as we noted early in our study, the spirit lies in the shadow of death: "When you hide your face [*pānîm*], they [the animals] are dismayed; when you take away their spirit [*rûaḥ*], they die and return to their dust." The uncomplicated exposé of life and death in Psalm 51 serves to explain the plea "Deliver me from bloodshed" in Psalm 51:14 (MT 51:16). Quite simply, the poet does not want to die, and the perennial presence of God's holy spirit, which lies within the poet, keeps him from doing so.

Essential to this penitential Psalm 51 are dimensions of God's spirit that are a matter of virtue. Renewal of spirit. Holiness of spirit. Readiness of spirit. Contrition of spirit. In Psalm 51, the inscrutable quality of *rûaḥ*, which finds no counterpart in the English language, crescendos. *Rûaḥ* is not mere breath, the physical animation of the body. Nor is *rûaḥ* primarily a gift of salvation tied to baptism or some other act of faith or ritual. *Rûaḥ* is the core—we might say the heart and soul—of a human being where God is particularly vigorous. God renews a steadfast spirit. God preserves a holy spirit. God establishes a ready spirit. God accepts a broken and contrite spirit.

Life is more than *rûaḥ* as breath. Life is more than *rûaḥ* as the source of salvation. Life, true life, vital life, robust life, is experienced with steadfastness, holiness, readiness, and contrition of spirit-breath. Those who live in this way—with every breath aimed at steadfastness, holiness, readiness, and brokenness—are alert and alive to God's presence-face (*pānîm*). This way of life is physical, yes. It is salvific too. Yet it is something more than either of these in isolation. It is a dogged devotion to cultivating a spirit that is steadfast, holy, ready, and broken. It is nurturing the sort of *rûaḥ* that God is poised to refresh, the sort of *rûaḥ* that God is inclined to sustain, the sort of *rûaḥ* that the poet knows God will never despise.

A New Heart and Spirit

Ezekiel is something of a marvel when it comes to the spirit. He adopts the word *rûaḥ* in contexts of weather and topography: a storm (Ezek. 1:4; 17:10; 19:12; 27:26), wind (5:10–12), and winds from the four corners of the earth (37:9) or simply the four directions of the compass (42:16–20). He uses the word with respect to human beings: the breath of living creatures (1:12, 20–21), strength (2:2; 3:24; 21:12) and spirit (3:14) in human beings, and the seat of thought (11:5; 20:32) akin to the human heart (14:4, 7), which has the potential, for Israel's prophets, to oppose divine inspiration (13:3). *Rûaḥ* can instill new life not just into individuals but into a moribund nation (37:1–14), upon which God promises to outpour *rûaḥ* (39:29). Ezekiel understands *rûaḥ* in his own experience as the force that falls upon him like the hand of God (8:1), causing him to speak (11:5). Finally, he claims frequently to have been transported by the spirit—presumably in visions—to Babylon to meet the exiles (3:14–15), back to Jerusalem to the temple's inner court (8:3), then to the temple's east gate (11:1) to watch the disheartening departure of the cherubim, and back again

to the exiles (11:24). Following Babylon's catastrophic decade of do-
minion in Jerusalem (597–587 BCE), he returns once more in a vision
to a meticulously restored and glory-laden temple, whose reality lies
in the near future (43:5).

All of this activity, frenzy even, is both enthralling and bewildering. Yet in the midst of it winds a strand of thought related to *rûaḥ*
that is simultaneously sane, challenging, and hopeful. This strand
occurs in Ezekiel 11:17–21, 18:30–32, and 36:25–26.

These three texts—variations on a theme—arise from different
periods of Ezekiel's life. To understand them, it is important to grasp
the basic lines of Ezekiel's life as a prophet, which cluster around
three significant events. In 597 BCE, Nebuchadnezzar of Babylon,
which was by now the dominant empire in the ancient Near East,
led a campaign to subdue Syria and Palestine. He took Judah's fickle
king Jehoiachin, along with other Judean leaders, into exile far away
in Babylon and set up Zedekiah as king.[7] Ezekiel was among those
exiles.

Four years later, in 593 BCE, while sitting alongside the River
Chebar in Babylon, Ezekiel experienced his call, which consisted of a
strange and vibrant series of visions of a mobile God on a throne that
looked more like a gyroscope than a chair (Ezek. 1–3). This image
of God proved revolutionary, just the ticket for a nation that had put
its faith in the temple. Many believed that, because God was in the
temple, no empire could launch a successful attack against Jerusalem.
Hymns such as Psalm 46 express the depth of this belief: "God is in
the midst of the city; it shall not be moved; God will help it when the
morning dawns. The nations are in an uproar, the kingdoms totter;
he utters his voice, the earth melts. The LORD of hosts is with us;
the God of Jacob is our refuge" (Ps. 46:5–7). Ezekiel's vision of God
undermined this image of a localized God and made it possible for
exiles in Babylon to continue worshiping the God of Israel far from
their homeland.

Then, sometime before 587 BCE, King Zedekiah of Judah rebelled
against Babylon. This time, Babylon was merciless. They devastated Jerusalem and sent many more "into exile" through forced

---

7. Details, scant though they be, can be found in 2 Kings 24:13–15.

deportation (2 Kings 25:21). Ezekiel records one of Judah's laments from this awful era: "Our bones are dried up, and our hope is lost; we are cut off completely" (Ezek. 37:11).

Ezekiel's prophetic voice can be divided into two periods. For six or seven years (from 593 until roughly 587 BCE), he said and did all he could to convince his countrymen and -women to purify the temple, to sanitize the priesthood, and to clean up their act by yielding to Israel's God rather than imperial powers. He was unsuccessful. Still, rather than licking his wounds and claiming that he had warned everyone, he turned after the fall of Jerusalem in 587 BCE to set about the task of giving people hope. For six years or so Ezekiel tried to break through the false assurance that God would protect Jerusalem; then Ezekiel spent the rest of his life after 587 BCE trying to wrest hope from despair.

There was more than enough despair to go around, even in Ezekiel's early period of prophecy. As the Babylonian noose tightened around Israel's neck, some people naturally, perhaps justifiably, raised the question of responsibility in the form of a proverb: "The parents have eaten sour grapes, and the children's teeth are set on edge" (Ezek. 18:2).[8] Why should children suffer for their parents' mistakes? Ezekiel responded by demonstrating at length that each individual's sin or act of obedience determines his or her destiny. This lengthy response to the maxim concludes with a challenge:

> Cast away from you all the transgressions that you have committed against me, and make yourselves a new heart and a new spirit! Why will you die, O house of Israel? For I have no pleasure in the death of anyone, says the Lord GOD. Turn, then, and live. (Ezek. 18:31–32 alt.)

Ezekiel commands the people to *make for themselves* a new heart and spirit. These are experiences the Israelites can bring about themselves, a condition they can ensure. They can cast away their transgressions. Ezekiel argues that each individual has it under his or her own control

---

8. Ezekiel's older contemporary Jeremiah also quotes this maxim: "In those days they shall no longer say: 'The parents have eaten sour grapes, and the children's teeth are set on edge.' But all shall die for their own sins; the teeth of everyone who eats sour grapes shall be set on edge" (Jer. 31:29–30).

not only to repent but to develop in themselves a new heart and a new spirit. This command is hardly startling. We have seen virtuous Israelites—Joseph, Moses, and Daniel among them—whose dogged discipline led them to be identified as people with God's spirit within them. In essence, they made for themselves hearts of wisdom.

Yet there is a twist in Ezekiel's promise. Renewal is not a matter of refreshment or transformation. Renewal is a matter of *replacement*. Only a new heart and a new spirit will do. Yet, surprisingly perhaps, Ezekiel does not lay responsibility for these replacement parts at the feet of God. Each individual can stop sinning and make for himself or herself a new heart. Ezekiel apparently has an optimism, at least at this early stage, that individuals can determine their own destiny. Children should stop complaining about how their teeth are set on edge. They should grit their teeth instead, cast away sin, and make for themselves a new heart and spirit.

Ezekiel returns to this theme later, but still before the destruction of Jerusalem in 587 BCE, in a series of visions in which the sins of the still-standing temple become progressively more grotesque (Ezek. 8–11). The priests have made a muck of the temple with their hidden sins and misplaced loyalties—they apparently hedged their bets—to Babylonian gods. Despite the disgust he feels at the sins that cause the glorious cherubim to fly away from the temple, Ezekiel musters the ability to promise a fresh ingathering of exiles with one heart and a new spirit within:

> Thus says the Lord GOD: I will gather you from the peoples, and as-semble you out of the countries where you have been scattered, and I will give you the land of Israel. When they come there, they will remove from it all its detestable things and all its abominations. I will give them one heart, and put a new spirit within them; I will remove the heart of stone from their flesh and give them a heart of flesh, so that they may follow my statutes and keep my ordinances and obey them. Then they shall be my people, and I will be their God. (Ezek. 11:17–20)

Despite horrific temple abominations, Ezekiel is still hopeful that the people can ultimately have a future. Once they have removed the causes of sin, God will respond by giving to the restored exiles a single heart and a new spirit to enable them to be fully God's people, completely obedient. Yet something has changed since Ezekiel first issued this promise. A new heart and spirit are no longer a product of human initiative; they are now divine gifts. Although Babylon is breathing down Judah's neck, Ezekiel still holds out hope.

This hope is not exclusively Ezekiel's own. His contemporary Jeremiah held out a similar hope. Jeremiah promised a new covenant that God would "make with the house of Israel after those days, says the LORD: I will put my law within them, and I will write it on their hearts; and I will be their God, and they shall be my people" (Jer. 31:33). Ezekiel and Jeremiah shared a vision of the future, though only Ezekiel attributed that future to a new spirit.

Ezekiel's hope is not for renewal or transformation, like the hope of Psalm 51. God again acts surgically, replacing Israel's heart of stone with a heart of flesh and placing a new spirit within Israel. God's work is also clinical. Gone is the kneeling in the dust and breathing life into the face of the first human; now God instead *places rûaḥ* within Israel. The image is a tidier one.

Command (Ezek. 18:30–32) and promise (11:17–20) reappear a third time—this time *after* the fall of Jerusalem. The early versions, both expressed before the catastrophe of 587 BCE, share a conviction: the Israelites are capable of putting away their sins and setting aside their idols. In the third version, the sinister side of Israel's character—with the rubble of Jerusalem taken as evidence—rules out human initiative:

> I will take you from the nations, and gather you from all the countries, and bring you into your own land. I will sprinkle clean water upon you, and you shall be clean from all your uncleannesses, and from all your idols I will cleanse you. A new heart I will give you, and a new spirit I will put within you; and I will remove from your body the heart of stone and give you a heart of flesh. I will put my spirit within you, and make you follow my statutes and be careful to observe my ordinances. Then you shall live in the land that I gave to your ancestors; and you shall be my people, and I will be your God. (Ezek. 36:24–28)[9]

---

9. This promise has not emerged from thin air but out of Ezekiel's fidelity to the Deuteronomic tradition:

> When all these things have happened to you, the blessings and the curses that I have set before you, if you call them to mind among all the nations where

In the aftermath of Jerusalem's demise, hope is different. *Darker*. God cannot simply promise that Israel will be restored to the land, for there is little good in a collection of Israelites whose earlier actions led to the destruction of Jerusalem. Exiled Israel can no longer be asked to repent (11:14–21) or to make for themselves a new heart and a new spirit (18:30–32). They had their chance and showed themselves incapable.

A new element shows up, therefore, in this final version of Ezekiel's promise of a new heart and spirit: *the imperative of cleansing*. God will purify Israel with water sprinkled over them. This looks like a gentle image—sprinkling with water. It is not. Nearly every occurrence of the verb *sprinkle* in the books of Torah pictures the blood of slaughtered animals dashed or thrown against the altar.[10] This cleansing is wrenching, violent even, reminiscent, ironically enough, of the animal sacrifices in the tent of meeting and, more painfully, of the sacrifices that no longer take place in Jerusalem in Ezekiel's day, since the temple lies in ruins because of Israel's sins.[11] Israel needs water not so much sprinkled upon them as splattered all over them.

Once this is done, God will do what God promised before: take away Israel's heart of stone and replace it with a heart of flesh. Then, as if to punctuate the promise, God promises *twice* to put God's

---

the LORD your God has driven you, and return to the LORD your God, and you and your children obey him with all your heart and with all your soul, just as I am commanding you today, then the LORD your God will restore your fortunes and have compassion on you, gathering you again from all the peoples among whom the LORD your God has scattered you. Even if you are exiled to the ends of the world, from there the LORD your God will gather you, and from there he will bring you back. The LORD your God will bring you into the land that your ancestors possessed, and you will possess it; he will make you more prosperous and numerous than your ancestors. (Deut. 30:1–5)

Although Ezekiel is faithful to this tradition, the dire situation brought about by the fall of Jerusalem propels him to transpose this tradition into a higher key. While Deut. 30 promises restoration *without* cleansing, Israel's experience evokes from Ezekiel a more radical solution of purification: "I will sprinkle clean water upon you, and you shall be clean from all your uncleannesses, and from all your idols I will cleanse you" (Ezek. 36:25).

10. E.g., Exod. 29:16, 20; Lev. 1:5, 11; 2 Kings 16:13; 2 Chron. 29:22.

11. Worship seems to have continued during this era in Mizpah, several miles north of Jerusalem. You will find a brief sketch of life in Palestine and Babylon in my *The Holy Spirit before Christianity* (Waco: Baylor University Press, 2019), 138–41, 220–21nn59–78.

spirit within Israel—a spirit that will inspire Israel to follow God's statutes and observe God's ordinances.

In all three of these expressions, Ezekiel plays with tradition. Deuteronomy promises that God will circumcise Israel's heart (Deut. 30:6). For Ezekiel, circumcision will not do; a new heart altogether is necessary. Yet not just a new heart—a new heart *and a new spirit*. This development of the Deuteronomic tradition is fresh. Hammered on the anvil of Israel's recalcitrance (Ezek. 11:24–31; 18:30–32), it yields a promise (36:25–26) that paves the way for Ezekiel's vision of the inbreathing of the valley of dry bones, which ends, "I will put my spirit-breath within you, and you shall live, and I will place you on your own soil; then you shall know that I, the LORD, have spoken and will act" (37:14 alt.).

Ezekiel, for years isolated from his own people because of his criticism of the priesthood, the temple, and the monarchy, still manages to unearth hope for them, even in a desert from which life has vanished. That loss of life creates the opportunity in the aftermath of destruction for God to give Israel a new spirit that will inspire them to follow God's commandments—to live, in short, with a spirit that is the source of virtue.

Though separated by different concerns (individual sin and national guilt) and different genres (poetic lament and prophetic oracle), Psalm 51 and Ezekiel's prophecies share a conviction about the association of God's spirit with wisdom and virtue. In Psalm 51, the poet—an individual—prays for the creation of a new heart and the renewal of a right spirit. Ezekiel, the prophet, offers, by way of command and promise, a new heart and a new spirit to inspire an entire community to return to God's commands. Hope for obedience in Ezekiel's prophecy resonates with the poet's hope for a right, ready, and holy spirit.

To attain this level of holiness demands a work of God, yet that work is not static in the Jewish Scriptures. In the story of how deftly Israel constructed a tabernacle in the desert, God filled the wise of heart with a *rûaḥ* of wisdom (Exod. 28:3; 35:30–35). The artisans needed neither a renewed spirit nor a new one. Their hearts and spirits were wise already, finely honed, and they needed only to have their spirits full to the brim with wisdom in order to accomplish the prodigious task of constructing a portable place of worship in the unremitting harshness of the desert. The psalm, in contrast, bleeds with penitence and the desire for a *renewed* heart and spirit. Nothing less, believes the poet, will stave off death and forestall the withdrawal of God's face. Ezekiel, more flamboyant than both the storyteller and the poet, goes a step further when he yearns for a *replacement* heart and spirit for the *whole* of Israel, since theirs is rotten to the core. Not a spirit topped up or a spirit renewed but a new spirit altogether is ultimately the only solution that will do for a doomed nation. Ezekiel knows that Israel needs cleansing. Not a gentle rain, a mist, but a scrubbing, a splattering, a spraying of water—and a wrenching reminder of sacrifices now long gone.

In this conviction, Ezekiel is hardly alone. The poet whose legacy lies in the deep remorse expressed by Psalm 51 knows this too. He launches a volley across the divine bow by twice begging God to *blot out* sins (Ps. 51:1, 9; MT 51:3, 11). Absent any sense of protocol or propriety, the poet dives in with a dual demand—no time for pleasantries and politeness—for a thorough washing from iniquity, the way one scrubs a filthy cloak,[12] and for a cleansing from sin, the way the infirm are purified after being healed[13] (51:2; MT 51:4). He pleads for purging with hyssop and scrubbing until he is whiter than snow (51:7; MT 51:9). Both pleas are striking by dint of their oddity; hyssop typically does not grow in Palestine, and snow is rarely to be seen. These prayers tumble over one another; the guilt and grief-ridden poet fumbles over his words, repeating himself, pitifully pleading again and again for the same thing: a copious scrubbing until he is finally clean inside and out. "Squeaky clean," as my mother used to say, on those rare occasions when I took a bath. Nothing less will do. The poet, exhausted from sin, begs ad nauseam to be clean again.

---

12. For example, Exod. 19:10–14; Lev. 6:20–17:16 (twenty-seven times).
13. For example, Lev. 13:6–59.

8

Spirit Standing and Guiding

> Before reading this chapter, explore these texts:
>
> » Isaiah 63:7–19
> » Haggai 2:1–9

With deep devotion Israel hung its fate, like harps on exilic willows, on the conviction that God was present and active from the beginning, when a rabble of slaves ascended out of Egypt. Israel saw God obliquely but unmistakably at the cusp of liberation from Egypt.

This belief was foundational not only in times of achievement and affluence but in eras of destitution and despair. During those bouts with despair, *especially* those times, Israel remembered how they had eked out an existence at the whim of an ancient empire— only to escape one day. Their escape—their *exodus*—was wonderful, miraculous even, but it led them to a terrifying wilderness, where they wandered for years on end, burning out the light of an

---

I recently devoted a book to this topic, *The Holy Spirit before Christianity* (Waco: Baylor University Press, 2019).

entire generation. Yet as they remembered the story later, they had not wandered alone. God was inevitably, incontrovertibly present in a menagerie of mysterious entities that led them along the way. There were pillars of cloud by day and fire by night, clouds that lifted and descended on them, a terrifying angel to lead the way. Even a strange face, like the *pānîm* of a god, led them—until the ragtag band reached a land flowing with milk and honey, where they lived, if not happily, at least with intermittent solace, for centuries.

Even as they remembered these early traumatic days of peril and provision, Israel nursed a tandem belief that God was present with them as *rûaḥ*. As we have seen time and again, for more than half a millennium (from eighth-century prophets Hosea, Micah, and Isaiah to the book of Daniel, which was written in response to the horrors of Antiochus IV Epiphanes), Israelite and Jewish authors embraced the presence, power, and promise of *rûaḥ*.

These two swaths of tradition—exodus and *rûaḥ*—merged during the Babylonian and Persian eras (between 587 and 445 BCE) in two slender slices of prophetic literature: Haggai 2:4–5 and Isaiah 63:7–14. This combination marked an unprecedented development in Israel's understanding of the spirit.

The measure of this merger can be illustrated by an experience my wife, Priscilla, and I had in 1989 when we traveled to Scotland's Orkney Islands. On a cold, gray morning at the ferry terminal in John o' Groats at the northeastern tip of Scotland, we drank coffee and ate chocolate-covered rice krispie treats. On the ferry, I lost both. The route from the Scottish mainland to the Orkney Islands took us directly into the path where the North Sea and the Atlantic Ocean collide. We sailed along that seam where these two great forces meet. The meeting of the Atlantic Ocean and North Sea is akin to what happened during the Babylonian and Persian eras of Israel's history, when spirit and exodus—two great oceans of tradition— met with exceptional results (far less ludicrous than my experience in Scotland).[1]

---

1. My *Holy Spirit before Christianity* makes the case for this unprecedented development.

Agents of the Exodus

Through the mists of communal reminiscence, Israel clung doggedly to the conviction that God had acted along the shores of the sea, in the desert, at the storied mountain, and on the eastern banks of the Jordan River. The conviction that God was present then, if not in their own latter-day turmoil, circulated in Israel's bloodstream. *How* God was present was not easily answered, but Israel held on to that conviction by remembering various agents who were active in the long haul from Egypt to the promised land: pillars of fire and cloud, an extraordinary angel, and the presence or face or presence-face—the *pānîm*—of God.

From the start, God's guidance lay principally in pillars; at least, that is where Israel's memory first pinpointed divine guidance of the slaves as they fled.

> The LORD was traveling in front of them in a pillar of cloud by day, to lead them along the way, and in a pillar of fire by night, to give them light, so that they might travel by day and by night. Neither the pillar of cloud by day nor the pillar of fire by night left its place in front of the people. (Exod. 13:21–22 alt.)

These pillars are the baseline of God's presence. The rest of Jewish Scripture offers variations on this theme, but at this point at least, the nature of God's presence in two pillars is straightforward and solid: God traveled in pillars by day and night.

Yet before the escapees managed to get anywhere, the Egyptian army cornered them, hedging them in between the Egyptian camp and the sea. The night before liberation, the two pillars seemed to merge into one pillar of fire and cloud and stopped by the shores of the sea: "The angel of God who was going before the Israelite army moved and went behind them; and the pillar of cloud moved from in front of them and took its place behind them. It came between the army of Egypt and the army of Israel. And so the cloud was there with the darkness, and it lit up the night; one did not come near the other all night" (Exod. 14:19–20). This is a strange development. Gone are the simple days when God traveled in front of itinerant Israel in a pillar of cloud and a pillar of fire. The pillars are now one, and that pillar has now stopped, along with an angel, to guard Israel by lighting up the night.

Then, with the Egyptian chariots and horses in hot pursuit, "at the morning watch the LORD in the pillar of fire and cloud looked down upon the Egyptian army, and threw the Egyptian army into panic" (Exod. 14:24). Once again, the two have become one. Whether God is atop the pillar, in it, or behind it, may not be possible to say. Yet God looks *through* it. This pillar is the window through which God looks in order to send Egypt into a panic.[2] Again, then, God is associated with the pillars—this time, *one* pillar—so intimately that God is able to watch Egypt through it, as through an old-fashioned keyhole.

The Israelites did not tidy these memories when they collected them in writing. Whether it was one pillar or two, whether they stood or traveled—these are not paramount issues. *That* the pillars traveled, *that* they protected the refugees, *that* God was in the pillar(s)—these are the essential convictions of Israel's memories of God's presence in the early days long before they lived in the land of promise.

■   ■   ■

The pillar was not the only agent to stand guard on that harrowing night before the exodus. "The angel of God who was going before the Israelite army moved and went behind them; and the pillar of cloud moved from in front of them and took its place behind them" (Exod. 14:19). The angel moved from front to rear, from fore to aft, along with the pillar. The angel is somewhat superfluous in this scenario; the pillar does the guarding. What the angel does is not yet obvious.

Later in the story, with Israel safely entrenched at Mount Sinai, what the angel is to do becomes crystal clear:

> I [God] am going to send an angel in front of you, to guard you on the way and to bring you to the place that I have prepared. Be attentive to him and listen to his voice; do not rebel against him, for he will not pardon your transgression; for my name is in him.

2. In Gen. 26:8, the king of the Philistines looked through the window and saw Isaac "playing with" Rebekah. In 2 Kings 9:30, 32, Jezebel saw Jehu through the window, while he saw her through the window.

But if you listen attentively to his voice and do all that I say, then I will be an enemy to your enemies and a foe to your foes.

When my angel goes in front of you, and brings you to the Amorites, the Hittites . . . (Exod. 23:20–23)

The actions of the angel are inescapable—and of enormous benefit to Israel—described as they are by a series of key verbs. The angel will *protect* Israel on the journey; what it offered on that first propitious night along the shores of the sea, it now provides perpetually. The angel will *bring* them to the place God has prepared; the angel, in short, will finish the job begun in Egypt. The angel will *speak* to the Israelites; God commands them to "listen attentively to his voice." The angel will *travel in front of* the Israelites; the prerogatives of God and the pillars, here at least, belong equally to the angel.

Slightly later, and twice in close succession, God reiterates this promise: "My angel shall go in front of you" (Exod. 32:34). Then, in the wake of a short-lived but devastating plague prompted by Israel's effort to create a golden calf (because they grew impatient with Moses, who lingered with God too long on Mount Sinai), God promises again, "I will send an angel before you, and I will drive out the Canaanites, the Amorites, the Hittites, the Perizzites, the Hivites, and the Jebusites" (33:2). No measure of Israelite recalcitrance can prompt God to withdraw this promise.

When God repeats the promise of the angel, this reiteration comes with a wicked twist, as is so often the case in biblical repetition. God promises the guidance of an angel yet again—but with that promise comes God's refusal to lead Israel any farther: "I will send an angel before you," pledges God, "but I will not go up among you, or I would consume you on the way, for you are a stiff-necked people" (Exod. 33:2–3). The angel will go with Israel, but God will not. The promise of *God's* angel becomes now the promise of an angel *without God*. This promise, therefore, is an ominous sign in its third occurrence.

It is not just an ominous sign in the abstract, a sort of premonition. The altered promise becomes the basis for an intense conversation between God and Moses. *Conversation* is probably the wrong word. *Negotiation* is better. *Tense negotiation* is better yet.

Before Moses gets a word in edgewise to protest this backhanded promise, two scenes occur. In the first, the Israelites repent for the golden calf debacle (Exod. 33:4–6). The second scene describes how Moses would regularly meet God outside the camp at the tent of meeting, where the pillar of God would descend, and speak to God as a friend (33:7–11). This note of camaraderie vanishes quickly when Moses and God square off. In a tangled and tortured conversation, Moses begs God to accompany Israel; he urges God to "consider too that this nation is your people" (33:13). The angel, Moses implies, will simply not do. Surprisingly, divine acquiescence is immediate: "My presence-face [*pānîm*] will go with you, and I will give you rest" (33:14).

Acquiescence may be immediate—but it is inadequate from where Moses stands. God fails to include Israel in the promise of divine presence. In the promise, God refers only to Moses here with a singular *you*: my presence will give you, Moses, rest. So Moses demands again that the compass of God's care extend to the people: "If your presence-face [*pānîm*] will not go, do not carry *us* up from here. For how shall it be known that I have found favor in your sight, *I and your people*, unless you go with *us*? In this way, *we* shall be distinct, *I and your people*, from every people on the face of the earth" (33:15–16, italics added). Moses's point is clear, emphatic, unambiguous: it is either everyone or no one.

Moses's strategy seems to work. God relents yet again: "I will do the very thing that you have asked" (33:17).

Still, it is not yet time for a sigh of relief. This is not the end of the conversation. Tension thickens the air when Moses demands, "Show me your glory, I pray" (Exod. 33:18), to which God responds, oddly enough, with a willingness to show Moses God's goodness, combined with another refusal: "you cannot see my presence-face [*pānîm*]; for no one shall see me and live" (33:20). That is that—except that this is a fierce negotiation, so what seems like the end of the story is not. Having reneged several times, God now relents, cradling Moses while the glory Moses requested passes by. Once God takes God's hand away, Moses does see—not God's presence-face [*pānîm*] but what lies *behind* God. Moses sees God from behind (33:21–23).

There is an exacting realism in this negotiation. Both God and Moses jockey for position. God issues threats and promises, reneges on both, and concedes parts of both. Moses makes demands of his own, pressing for every advantage, without winning ground. In the end, what is left is not clear. Has Moses seen God's glory? God's presence-face [*pānîm*]? Or neither? And how can God's presence-face accompany the people without being seen?

When the dust settles, a new agent of the exodus has emerged: God's presence-face or *pānîm*. Whether Moses ever sees this presence-face—Israel as a whole apparently does not—we may never know. But the presence-face may now be added to the growing coterie of agents who led the Israelites out of slavery and into a land of promise.

It is difficult to leave this passionate negotiation without a sigh of relief. If we have read it attentively, we have read it with bated breath. How this heated exchange is like speaking face-to-face with a friend is hard to imagine. This negotiation, rather, marks the height of tension, the apex of confusion, that permeates the tradition of God's accompaniment during Israel's early years. Did God journey with them (Exod. 13:21–22; 33:2–3)? Were there two pillars (13:21–22) or one (14:19–20; 33:9–10) or one made up of both cloud and fire (14:24)? Or was there a cloud that would luminesce at times—or luminesce constantly but be visible only in the darkness (14:19–20)? What was the primary purpose of the pillar(s)? To guide and guard Israel (13:21–22; 14:19–20, 24) or to descend on the tent outside the camp (33:9–10)? And what of the angel, whose initial gravitas diminishes in severity as Moses's penchant for the presence-face of God increases (14:19; 23:20–23; 32:34; 33:2–3, 14–15)?

The picture is full of overlap and ambiguity. No one sat down during the void of the Babylonian exile and ironed out the creases. No one returned to Palestine in 539 BCE and excised alternative traditions. No one censored allegedly obsolete ones. No one commented, "It wasn't two pillars; it was just one." No one wrote, "It wasn't an angel; it was a pillar." No one contended, "It wasn't a pillar; it was God's *pānîm* that led them." All of these agents jockeyed for attention in Israel's memory. All of these thrived not just on the surface but in the marrow of Israel's memory.

This memory—these memories—of agents of the exodus, disordered though it may have been, is the ancestral home of the holy spirit. Israel would change over the centuries through wrenching experiences but carry with it the essential conviction that God was present in an array of agents—even if that memory changed over the years too. An unprecedented change occurred no more dramatically than in two prophetic writings—Haggai 2:5 and Isaiah 63:7–14—to which it is possible to trace a new era in Israel's understanding of the spirit. The authors of these texts introduced the spirit into the traditions of the exodus, in which God had rescued Israel from Egypt through a cadre of divine agents—pillars, an angel, and God's own face or *pānîm*. What this move meant for Israel's conception of the spirit is nothing short of spectacular.

A Word of Assurance

"Work, for I am with you, says the LORD of hosts, according to the word that I cut with you when you came out of Egypt," urges Haggai (2:4–5).[3] He then adds promise to command, "My spirit stands among you; do not fear" (2:5 alt.). Though perhaps not at first blush, certainly at a second glance, this word of assurance is baffling. God spoke many words with Israel when they came out of Egypt: the Ten Words (Exod. 20:1–17); the designation of Israel as a kingdom of priests, holy and set apart (19:3–6); commands to follow; sacrifices to make; offerings to give; tents to build.

Word after word after word. Promise following command. Command following promise. Words for the whole community. Words whispered in secret just to Moses—some in the conviviality of companionship, others through gritted teeth. So many words spoken when they came out of Egypt.

Just not this one: *my spirit stands among you*. That word God did *not* say. That word God did *not* cut. That pledge God did *not* make when they came out of Egypt. Haggai refers to a promise that does not exist, at least not verbatim, anywhere in the Hebrew Bible.

3. This is my translation, which preserves the verb *cut* even though it creates an awkward English expression.

Another bewildering aspect of this reminiscence in Haggai 2:5 is that, among the nearly four hundred other references to *rûaḥ* in the Hebrew Bible, there is not a single one to *rûaḥ* standing. The spirit rushes upon, is upon, pours out, empties upon, blows, clothes, and rests upon—along with a host of other actions. But the spirit does not *stand*. Yet that is the word lying at the heart of Haggai's word of assurance.

Why Haggai adopted the word *stand* is not hard to determine. It evoked the spirit's presence at a particularly threatening moment in Israel's distant past when Israel came out of Egypt. Pinned between the Egyptian army and the sea, Israel faced annihilation. Yet pillars of cloud and fire accompanied them. All of a sudden, as evening set and peril reared its head:

> The angel of God who was going before the Israelite army moved and went behind them; and the pillar of cloud moved from in front of them and *stood* behind them. It came between the army of Egypt and the army of Israel. And so the cloud was there with the darkness, and it lit up the night; one did not come near the other all night. (Exod. 14:19–20, italics added)

The pillar of cloud *stood* between Israel and the Egyptian army and protected them on the cusp of escape. Without this movement from fore to aft, without the pillar's shift from guide to rear guard, Israel would never have crossed the sea, traversed the wilderness, and settled in the land of promise. This was a singular moment of salvation.

The word *pillar*, in fact, is built from the same Hebrew root as *to stand* or *to take one's place*. "And stood" is *wayya'ămōḏ*; "pillar" is *'ammûḏ*. Verb and noun share the same Hebrew root, *'mḏ*. When, therefore, Haggai promises that the spirit stands in Israel's midst, he does not choose a verb cavalierly; Haggai 2:5 evokes both the verb *stand* and the noun *standing pillar* in the exodus story.

With this word, which he claims God cut—the word *cut* evokes the Hebrew idiom of cutting a covenant—with Israel when they came out of Egypt, Haggai recalls the pillars at the exodus. And for good reason. The inhabitants of the new Persian province of Judah had not gotten the job done in the years following the end of exile in Babylon. Paralyzed by drought, preoccupied by self-interest (homes needed to be built more than a temple), confronted with a strange new land they had never before seen (they were not exiled; their grandparents and great-grandparents were), and facing a precarious political Persian landscape they had never before known (with a governor rather than a king), they hesitated. It is difficult not to empathize with their hesitation, given needs that may have seemed, to them at least, more pressing than a shrine or sanctuary.

In short, they were afraid. Afraid of scarcity. Afraid of the threat posed by others in the land. Afraid of Persia, with its new policy of allowing exiles to return home but without restoration of the monarchy. So Haggai transforms the first exodus into *their* exodus: *my spirit stands among you*. Past and present fold together in Haggai's promise. The people of the restoration are the people of the exodus. The people fleeing Babylonian captivity are the people who fled Egypt. Haggai's people, not just a generation long past, are the recipients of God's word, the object of God's protection.

For Haggai, there is no palpable pillar to which he can point during the early years of rebuilding after Persian ruler Cyrus's mandate to return and rebuild, no corporeal cloud that exists to signal God's presence. But there is something else that can stand in Israel's midst and signal God's protection. There is spirit, *rûaḥ*, standing like the pillars on the shore of the sea in order to stay the hand of enemies perceived or real.

The Agony of Lament

In the harshness of the crises posed by geopolitical shifts, not least Babylon's mercurial rise and precipitous fall to Persia, Israel had the option of jettisoning their traditions, of dismissing them as unrealistic, unattainable, entirely forgettable. They took another tack by evaluating their own failure in light of those traditions, and in a move that proved indispensable for their understanding of the spirit, they reinvented those traditions in the teeth of disappointment, even despair. Creativity rather than capitulation, vitality rather than evisceration, ruled the day, at least in the writings that survived the tumultuous sixth and fifth centuries.

One of those creative appropriations of Israel's tradition occurs in an unobtrusive lament:

> In all their distress, the angel of his presence saved them;[4]
> in his love and in his pity he redeemed them;
> > he lifted them up and carried them all the days of old.
>
> But they rebelled
> > and grieved [or rebelled against] his holy spirit;
> therefore he became their enemy;
> > he himself fought against them.
> Then they remembered the days of old,
> > of Moses his servant.
> Where is the one who brought them up out of the sea
> > with the shepherds of his flock?
> Where is the one who put within them
> > his holy spirit,
> who caused his glorious arm
> > to march at the right hand of Moses,
> who divided the waters before them
> > to make for himself an everlasting name,
> > who led them through the depths?
> Like a horse in the desert,
> > they did not stumble.
> Like cattle that go down into the valley,
> > the spirit of the LORD gave them rest.
> Thus you led your people,
> > to make for yourself a glorious name. (Isa. 63:9–14)

This lament contains several allusions to the exodus tradition. The first occurs in the unique phrase *the angel of his presence*. This simple phrase is actually a creative amalgamation of two figures from Israel's traditions: the angel of the exodus and God's presence-face or *pānîm*.

Before looking more closely at this phrase, it is important to note that the Hebrew text and its Greek translation differ from one

---

4. This line, from Isa. 63:9, is my translation, based upon the Hebrew text. NRSV, in contrast, is based primarily on the Greek translation, the Septuagint.

another. The Hebrew reads: "In all their distress, the angel of his presence saved them." The Greek translators opted instead for this: "It was no ambassador or angel but the Lord himself that saved them." The Greek translators took the opposite interpretation of the Hebrew—it was *not* an angel that saved Israel—perhaps because they were reluctant to attribute salvation to an angel rather than to God.

It was not unusual for the Greek translators to eliminate difficulties in Hebrew texts. For example, Genesis 2:4 in the Hebrew says that God completed God's work on the seventh day. This implies that God violated the Sabbath by working on the seventh day—God *completed* the work on the seventh day. The Greek translators solved this problem with a tweak by simply changing seventh to sixth: God completed God's work on the *sixth* day, the Greek translation says. Then God rested on the seventh.

There are good reasons for accepting that the Hebrew of Isaiah 63:9 represents the original text, not least that Greek translators might not have wanted to credit an angel rather than God with the exodus.[5] It is in the Hebrew that the significance of the phrase *angel of his presence* surfaces.

We saw already that God promised Israel an angel with divine authorization—God's name was in the angel—to lead them to the promised land. Later, in a tense tête-à-tête with Moses, God distanced the angel from God's own leading. The angel would go, but God would not. This led God to offer God's presence or *pānîm*, though it is never clear whether God made good on this promise.

This negotiation between God and Moses, for all its intensity, resolves little and, arguably, raises more questions than it settles. From the start, the relationship between the angel and the presence-face (*pānîm*) is vague. The angel was inferior, at least to Moses's mind, but how inferior is simply not clear. Accompanying this question is another: whether the angel or the presence-face (*pānîm*) of God would accompany Israel as a whole—or just Moses.

These questions go unanswered in Moses's dialogue with God in Exodus 33. *Which* will accompany, God's angel or presence-face (*pānîm*)?

---

5. This is a complicated issue, which I have discussed at length in an excursus, "The Dubious Preference for Greek Isaiah 63:7–14" in *Holy Spirit before Christianity*, 134–37, 219–20nn46–58.

Whom will that angel or presence-face accompany, Moses or the whole people? These questions are left to languish in Israel's memory of the sojourn at Sinai. None comes to a tolerably clear conclusion.

In one fell swoop, the prophet of lament who penned Isaiah 63:7–14 resolves this tension between the angel and God's presence-face: the angel *of* God's presence rescued them from Egypt. These two figures—God's angel and God's presence—which compete in the book of Exodus, become one and the same agent in the Hebrew of Isaiah 63: *the angel of God's presence*. This lament also answers the question of *whom* the angel of God's presence will lead: "the angel of his presence saved *them*; in his love and in his pity he redeemed *them*; he lifted *them* up and carried *them* all the days of old." The angel of God's presence liberated not just Moses but the whole of Israel from Egypt. The point of negotiation that drove Moses to distraction, whether God would accompany all of God's people, is neatly settled in this lament.

This is only the beginning of the metamorphosis that occurs in this lament. More emerges in what follows. The alchemy that blended the angel and presence-face of God emerges now in a peculiar fusion of that angel with the holy spirit, as the prophet recollects how Israel

> rebelled
> > and grieved his holy spirit;
> therefore he became their enemy;
> > he himself fought against them. (Isa. 63:10)

A clear sequence is in this portion of the lament—from the angel of God's presence to God's holy spirit. Yet there is more, in fact, than sequence joining angel and spirit at the hip. There is an identification of the angel of God's presence with God's holy spirit. This is apparent in the initial verb associated with this holy spirit—*rebelled*—which has its roots in the first promise of the *angel* delivered at Mount Sinai. What is said of God's holy spirit in the lament was said earlier of God's angel in the divine promise in which God warned Israel not to rebel against the promised angel: "Be attentive to him and listen to his voice; do not rebel against him, for he will not pardon your transgression; for my name is in him" (Exod. 23:21).

What characterized the promise of Haggai now characterizes the prophetic lament. The spirit has taken on the role of an agent in the exodus tradition. For Haggai, this agent is the pillar that had stood in Israel's midst. Now, assures Haggai, the spirit stands among those who must rebuild the temple, so there is no need to be afraid. For Isaiah 63, this is the angel of God's presence against which Israel was warned not to rebel; now, laments the prophet, Israel has rebelled against God's holy spirit. The angel of God's presence and the holy spirit are one and the same.

Just a few lines later, the prophet raises further lament:

> Where is the one who brought them up out of the sea
>   with the shepherds of his flock?
> Where is the one who put within them
>   his holy spirit,
> who caused his glorious arm
>   to march at the right hand of Moses,
> who divided the waters before them
>   to make for himself an everlasting name,
>   who led them through the depths?
>   (Isa. 63:11–12)

Wedged into this context and its preoccupation with deliverance through the sea is the plea, "Where is the one who put within them his holy spirit?" The difficulty with this question is simply that God did *not* put the holy spirit within Israel during deliverance through the sea—not at least according to the exodus story itself. The agents of deliverance were the pillar and the angel, which "moved and went behind them" to shelter them from the advancing Egyptian army (Exod. 14:19). On the eve of liberation, the angel moved from helm to hind, setting itself in Israel's midst as a rear guard. The angel and the pillar protected Israel, making rescue through the sea possible the following day.

The transposition of the angel of God into the holy spirit is hardly sudden. Already the prophet has identified the angel of God's presence with God's holy spirit—and identified the holy spirit as the object of rebellion rather than the angel of Exodus 23. Now the prophet asks where that holy spirit is: "Where is the one who put within them his holy spirit" while Israel prepared to plow through the depths of the sea? Where is that angel now? Where is that holy spirit now? Where is that God now?

A final shift occurs in the last lines of this lament: "Like cattle that go down into the valley, the spirit of the LORD gave them rest" (Isa. 63:14). In these lines, the prophet yet again dips into the exodus tradition, this time to the entry into the promised land at the journey's end. And again there is a difficulty here: there is no place in the exodus tradition for a spirit that gave Israel rest. Yet again, the infamous negotiation between Moses and God, which is stubbornly and unforgettably wedged between two sets of stone tablets, provides a point of origin for the prophet's belief that "the spirit of the LORD gave them rest."

Deep into the negotiation, God tells Moses, "My presence-face [pānîm] will go with you, and I will give you rest." Moses reacts: "If your presence-face [pānîm] will not go, do not make us travel up from here" (Exod. 33:14–15). Only if God goes, argues Moses, will the uniqueness of Moses and the people be apparent to everyone on the face (pānîm)—the pun may be intentional—of the earth.

Permeating the to and fro of negotiation is an intimate association between the presence-face of God and rest: "My presence-face will go with you, and I will give you rest." This salient promise is the sole plausible precursor to the recollection in the lament, "the spirit of the LORD gave him [them] rest." What the presence-face of God was to accomplish in the exodus tradition—to give rest—the spirit now achieves in the later lament. Once again, the spirit has taken on the role of a guiding agent in the exodus tradition.

▬ ▬ ▬

This otherwise ordinary communal lament, tucked inconspicuously into the final chapters of Isaiah, contains a remarkable and unprecedented innovation in five steps:

1. The author merges two distinct agents of the exodus: the angel (Exod. 23:20–23; 32:34; 33:2) and God's presence (33:14–15). In Isaiah 63, the two become the angel *of* God's presence.

2. The author then shifts nearly imperceptibly from this angel to the holy spirit: "The angel of God's presence saved them . . . , but they rebelled against God's holy spirit."

3. The holy spirit takes on the role of the angel of the exodus. Rebellion against the angel in Exodus 23:21 becomes rebellion against the holy spirit in Isaiah 63:10.

4. The spirit is identified with the angel yet again as the one whom God put within Israel during the exodus in the question, "Where is the one who put within them his holy spirit?"

5. The spirit of the Lord takes on the role of the *pānîm* or presence-face of God. The rest God's presence or *pānîm* would give in Exodus 33 becomes the rest that the spirit of the Lord gave in Isaiah 63.

The magnitude of this innovation is enormous. For more than half a millennium, from eighth-century prophets to the book of Daniel, many Israelites embraced the power of *rûaḥ*. Prior to the composition of Haggai 2:4–5 and Isaiah 63:7–14, however, Israel's poets, prophets, and storytellers deemed the spirit to be active *but not an agent acting on God's behalf*. This scenario changed when the author of an otherwise typical communal lament at some point after 587 BCE and the prophet Haggai at some point after 539 BCE accomplished something unique.

Drawing on the exodus tradition, in which a pillar had stood in Israel's midst, Haggai encouraged his compatriots with the claim that now, centuries after the exodus, the spirit stood in *their* midst. Also drawing on the exodus tradition, a prophet of lament expanded the scope of the spirit. In this lament, the prerogatives of the agents of the exodus become the prerogatives of the spirit, God's *holy* spirit. Where the angel—now the angel of God's presence—once met with hostility, now the holy spirit is the object of rebellion. Where God had once set the angel in Israel's midst, now the holy spirit is within Israel. Where the *pānîm* had once been promised to give rest, now the spirit of the Lord gives Israel rest. Throughout Israel's Scriptures, the spirit blows and rushes upon and rests upon and outpours, yes, but none of these verbs captures the agency of the spirit, which emerged with salience, even exuberance, when Israel remembered the salvation wrought by the angel of God's presence and recalled how that salvation lay within the span of God's spirit.

This realization undercuts the convenient distinction between the spirit as a *power* in the first testament and a *person* in the second. That distinction might have held true had we halted our study at the last chapter. We might then have been able to document how Israelites conceived of the spirit as an impersonal force: blowing and inbreathing, rushing and resting upon, being distributed and passed on, outpouring, filling, and functioning as a source of purification and renewal. This possibility, consigning the spirit to the realm of the impersonal, evaporates in one prophet's lament and another's promise, in which the spirit—like the angel, pillars, and presence-face of God—stood within Israel and, once upon a time at least, led them to the promised land.

Conclusion

Standing there puzzling, gawking, and talking, talking, talking, Eliphaz the Temanite tells Job what Job does not want to hear, that what he, Eliphaz, has to say is inspired—though not in any ordinary way. Eliphaz's description is so supple, his impression so lithe, his admission so sincere, that we can almost forgive this otherwise unlikable man who drowns Job in defective reasoning to explain that Job sits there desolate, destitute, despairing on the ash heap day by day because he sinned. For a brief moment at least, Eliphaz becomes almost human. He tells Job how "a word came stealing to me," a whisper in the dark of night. It was dreadful, he admits, rattling his bones: "A spirit—a *rûaḥ*—glided past my face; the hair of my flesh bristled" (Job 4:12–15).

Goosebumps. Premonition. That momentary shudder in the face of something inscrutable, enigmatic, elusive. Like seeing a ghost. This is what Eliphaz felt in the eerie hours of the night. But what Eliphaz goes on to say about this spirit may be even more prescient: "It stood still, but I could not discern its appearance. A form was before my eyes" (Job 4:16). *I couldn't make it out, much as I tried.*

Then, something stranger still happens: "There was silence" (Job 4:16). Eliphaz knows—he seems to know little else worthwhile—that in the company of this spirit, this *rûaḥ*, lies sheer silence. Like the stillness after a violent storm.[1] Like a mantle-wrapped Elijah at the

---

1. The same noun occurs in Ps. 107:29.

cave after the earthquake, wind, and fire.[2] Silence. Sheer silence. *I couldn't make it out, much as I tried.*

It is the necessary fault of a book that it is filled with words when, occasionally at least, only silence will do. Goosebumps. Hair standing up on the nape of our necks. A shudder in the face of mystery, leaving us shaken, alert, alive—and terrified. That is the appropriate aftermath of a study of *rûaḥ* in the Jewish Scriptures.

I am wary, therefore, of tidying this book up. Three hundred eighty-nine or so unruly references to *rûaḥ* in the Jewish Scriptures make me hesitate—not dither or dawdle but pause. *I can't make it out, much as I try.*

This is a strange, ancient world we have entered, where a wind bearing quail is every bit as inspired as the spirit resting on seventy-two elders, stimulating them to prophesy. Where the spirit transgresses otherwise established boundaries by prompting a Babylonian seer's blessing of Israel. Where the spirit passes from mentor to protégé in a mantle. Where artisans are full to the brim of skill and spirit—both—so that they can construct a tent in the middle of nowhere. Where political leaders weep in genuine remorse over a crime committed. And where slave girls prophesy.

It is a real threat that tidying up these chapters will blunt the raw edge of mystery, imposing barriers where they do not exist and introducing taxonomies that do not suit. Yet it is also possible that we can garner the significance of this book by tracing lines loosely—*I can't make it out, much as I try.* These lines, if lightly held, may unmask defective categories, unsound assumptions, and unfounded conceptions and may lead ultimately to a more pliable and beneficial grasp of the elusive world of the spirit.

Beyond Definition

But where to start? The opening lines of the Jewish Scriptures offer an amenable point of departure: "In the beginning when God created the heavens and the earth, the earth was a formless void and darkness covered the face of the deep, while the *rûaḥ* of God swept over the

2. The same noun occurs in 1 Kings 19:12.

face of the waters" (Gen. 1:1–2). If we start at the start, we garner quite a few insights about *rûaḥ*.

As we have come to expect, the border between wind, breath, and spirit is porous. This is apparent in a variety of English translations. The NRSV reads, "a wind from God swept over the waters," and the CEB, "God's wind swept over the waters." The NIV has "the Spirit of God was hovering over the waters." *Rûaḥ*, of course, does mean "wind," but the phrase *rûaḥ 'ĕlōhîm* (*rûaḥ* of God) cannot easily be construed as a wind from God in light of the many other occurrences of the phrase in the Jewish Scriptures that are not casual references to a wind from God. Joseph, for example, has a spirit of God—*rûaḥ 'ĕlōhîm*—in him (Gen. 41:38), as do Bezalel and Oholiab, chief architects of the tabernacle who are filled with *rûaḥ 'ĕlōhîm* (Exod. 31:3; 35:31). The spirit of God comes upon Balaam (Num. 24:2) and Saul (1 Sam. 10:10, 20, 23; 11:6) alike, along with Azariah and Zechariah (2 Chron. 15:1; 24:20). Ezekiel's is the sole possible reference to a wind of God, though what lifts him is visionary and something other than an actual wind (Ezek. 11:24). To take *rûaḥ 'ĕlōhîm* in Genesis 1:2 as a wind from God, then, is to deviate from the basic connotation of the phrase in every other occurrence in the Jewish Scriptures.

Yet *Spirit* may not be quite right either. In every other instance of the phrase *rûaḥ 'ĕlōhîm*, an individual is mentioned on whom or in whom the spirit exists. The context of Genesis, by contrast, is cosmic, with waters and presumably winds.

Another possibility, too, rears its head: *rûaḥ* as breath. In this opening scene, God speaks word after word of creation; by speaking, God divides darkness from light, sea from land, day from night. The refrain "and God said" structures this opening poem in praise of the beauty and order of creation (Gen. 1:1–2:4). Breath, in other words, rolls over God's tongue in repeated acts of creation, of wresting beauty from the abyss. So *rûaḥ* in Genesis 1:2 may reflect the impending reality of divine breath.

Is *rûaḥ* wind? Spirit? Breath? Yes, and perhaps something more than each.

If translators lose the dynamic of the Hebrew word *rûaḥ*, it may not be their fault. It may be due to a difference in languages, a discrepancy in words. The Hebrew *rûaḥ* is richer and more resonant than the English words *breath*, *spirit*, or *wind*. English simply cannot shoulder the breadth of meaning that the original Hebrew and Aramaic languages of the Jewish Scriptures can. Though distinguishing between breath, wind, and spirit is necessary—sometimes the distinction is obvious in Hebrew—it is often a necessary evil that reduces the resonance of the Hebrew. The difference between Hebrew and English when it comes to *rûaḥ* is like the distinction between grand old college bells pealing in Oxford or Cambridge on any given Sunday morning and the clanging of a cowbell; both are bells, but each has its characteristic ring, with one decidedly preferable to the other (if being sonorous matters at all, which it does).

Beyond Gender

Another significant clue to the interpretation of *rûaḥ* lies in Genesis 1:2, in the verb *hover* or *sweep*, which prompted Eugene Peterson to translate this line in *The Message* as "God's spirit brooded like a bird above the watery abyss." The verb *hover*, which offers the first glimpse of the *rûaḥ*'s activity, occurs elsewhere in the Jewish Scriptures when God is portrayed as an eagle that "stirs up its nest, and hovers over its young;" this eagle "spreads its wings, takes them up, and bears them aloft on its pinions" (Deut. 32:11). The first word used to describe the action of *rûaḥ* in the Jewish Scriptures, then, occurs also in this description of a mother eagle.[3]

This realization, coupled with the feminine gender of the Hebrew word, may prompt a chorus of voices bent on identifying *rûaḥ* with the divine feminine, but the issue is not nearly as simple as that. The image of the mother eagle in Deuteronomy is, in a sense, a traditional view of the feminine. The mother protects her young, takes care of her babies, tends her offspring. From this point of view, *hovering* in Genesis 1—the Bible's opening lines—resonates with images of a mother hovering over a chaotic cosmic household. A few lines later God, her masculine counterpart, enters to shape order from chaos. (*"You wait until your father gets home!"*) She dithers; he is decisive.

3. In the Hebrew *piel* stem, it occurs only in these two texts; in the *qal* stem, it occurs also in Jer. 23:9, where it seems to refer to trembling.

Yet this first impression is the wrong impression. The word *hover* is only one of several verbs in Deuteronomy used to describe the liberation of Israel, the wilderness wandering, and the entry into the promised land:

> God sustained Israel in a desert land,
> in a howling wilderness waste;
> God shielded Israel, cared for Israel,
> guarded Israel as the apple of God's eye.
> As an eagle stirs up its nest,
> and hovers over its young;
> as it spreads its wings, takes them up,
> and bears them aloft on its pinions,
> the LORD alone guided Israel;
> no foreign God was with Israel.
> God set Israel atop the heights of the land,
> and fed Israel with produce of the field;
> God nursed Israel with honey from the crags,
> with oil from flinty rock. (Deut. 32:10–13 alt.)[4]

The verbs accompanying the mother eagle's hovering are anything but passive: sustain, shield, care for, guard, stir up, spread its wings, take up, bear aloft, guide, set atop, feed, and nurse. The mother eagle takes all sorts of initiative. She is a bird of prey grabbing her offspring with strong talons and powerful wings and lifting them up away from danger. This verb *hover* transcends the domestic and public spheres, obliterating traditional conceptions of feminine and masculine when it comes to God.

In this light, the first action of God's *rûaḥ* at the origin of the world encompasses spreading out, hovering, moving over the abyss. In its debut in the Bible's opening lines, the *rûaḥ* of God is like a mother eagle, a bird of prey. The spirit is not for this reason exclusively feminine any more than *rûaḥ* is exclusively masculine. Just as the word itself is more than breath, wind, or spirit, *rûaḥ* transcends simplistic notions of the feminine as maternal or relational and the

---

4. This text is difficult to translate because the Hebrew uses masculine verbs, but the operative image is the mother eagle. I substitute "God" for "he," and "Israel" for "him" in my translation of Deut. 32:10–13, using the NRSV as a base translation.

masculine as powerful or aggressive. There is, in fact, nothing inherently gendered in the spirit's resting upon or coming upon or clothing or filling or outpouring or guiding or standing, and it would be misguided to say there is. The rushing of the spirit on Samson is not, for example, masculine, and the resting of the spirit is not feminine; categories of gender cannot neatly be superimposed upon *rûaḥ* in the Jewish Scriptures. We should avoid projecting notions of femininity and masculinity on *rûaḥ*; the very first mention of *rûaḥ* in the Jewish Scriptures, which sets the agenda for the remaining references, is wholly unsuited to such projections.

Beyond Salvation

Genesis 1:2, as terse and opaque as it is, offers ample entrée to the world of *rûaḥ*. In light of the Bible's opening lines, *rûaḥ* transcends the trifurcation of breath, wind, and spirit; the bifurcation of male and female; and as we will now see, the dichotomy between creation and salvation.

Scattered statements that connect the spirit to salvation lie throughout the New Testament. The apostle Paul claims, for example, that "God's love has been poured into our hearts through the Holy Spirit that has been given to us" (Rom. 5:5). The pastoral letters contain unequivocal snippets condensing the act of salvation: "But when the goodness and loving kindness of God our Savior appeared, he saved us, not because of any works of righteousness that we had done, but according to his mercy, through the water of rebirth and renewal by the Holy Spirit. This Spirit he poured out on us richly through Jesus Christ our Savior" (Titus 3:4–6). The Gospel of John narrates the famed encounter between Nicodemus and the rabbi Jesus, in which Jesus instructs him, "Very truly, I tell you, no one can enter the kingdom of God without being born of water and Spirit. What is born of the flesh is flesh, and what is born of the Spirit is spirit" (John 3:5–6). By no means do all references connect the spirit to salvation, but enough do to suggest that the spirit is essential to the process of salvation.

This may be true, but a clear and present danger lies in the exclusive association of the spirit with salvation. In Christian theological terms, the *spiritus sanctificans* (the saving spirit) comes too easily to be separate from the *spiritus vivificans* (the life-giving spirit). The spirit that gives life, in short, is detached from the spirit that saves.

Several preeminent twentieth-century theologians have seen the peril in this distinction, none more urgently than Jürgen Moltmann, whose effort to connect *spiritus vivificans* and *spiritus sanctificans* has been tireless and, in an era of environmental change, prescient. "In both Protestant and Catholic theology and devotion," notes Moltmann,

> there is a tendency to view the Holy Spirit solely as *the Spirit of Redemption*. Its place is in the church, and it gives men and women the assurance of the eternal blessedness of their souls. This redemptive Spirit is cut off both from bodily life and from the life of nature. It makes people turn away from "this world" and hope for a better world beyond. They then seek and experience in the Spirit of Christ a power that is different from the divine energy of life, which according to the Old Testament ideas interpenetrates all the living.[5]

Moltmann recognizes that the Jewish Scriptures are essential for the obliteration of this false and potentially lethal dichotomy between creation and salvation. Progressive and promising theologies, notes Moltmann, "start from the Hebrew understanding of the divine Spirit and presuppose that the redeeming Spirit of Christ and the creative and life-giving Spirit of God are one and the same."[6] He goes on to say more urgently, "Faced with 'the end of nature,' the churches will either discover the cosmic significance of Christ and the Spirit, or they will share the guilt for the annihilation of God's earthly creation."[7]

Moltmann has pinpointed foundational insights about the spirit, even the spirit understood from a Christian vantage point, that are rooted in the Jewish Scriptures. To put it in more traditional terms, from the standpoint of the Old Testament, the spirit of salvation is none other than the spirit of creation. If we sequester these from each other and pay careful attention only to the spirit of salvation,

5. Jürgen Moltmann, *The Spirit of Life: A Universal Affirmation* (Minneapolis: Fortress, 1992), 8.
6. Moltmann, *Spirit of Life*, 9–10.
7. Moltmann, *Spirit of Life*, 10.

we doom our world—a world God so ably created and sustains—to annihilation.[8]

Another preeminent Christian theologian, Wolfhart Pannenberg, offers a comparable conception of the spirit. "According to the biblical testimony," claims Pannenberg,

> the Spirit of God is the life-giving principle, to which all creatures owe life, movement, and activity. This is particularly true of animals, plants, and humans, of which Psalm 104:30 says: "Thou sendest forth thy Spirit; they are created, and thou renewest the face of the ground." In keeping with this is the second creation account, which says that God "formed man of dust from the ground, and breathed into his nostrils the breath of life, and man became a living being" (Gen. 2:7; cf. Job 33:4). Conversely, all life perishes when God withdraws his Spirit (Ps. 104:29; Job 34:14f.). The souls of all living things and the breath of all people are in the hands of the Spirit (Job 12:10).[9]

These claims about the spirit of life—*rûaḥ*—are clear enough in the Jewish Scriptures. What Moltmann and Pannenberg demonstrate is how indispensable the Jewish Scriptures are to a full and rich experience of the spirit, an experience untrammeled by feeble and failing dichotomies.

Beyond Death

Before the drama of human history unravels, the Jewish Scriptures tell the tragic tale of two lovers. The intimacy of a potter-God's lips pressed against a freshly formed human figure, poised to blow breath within, brings the promise of unending love (Gen. 2:7). This

8. Jürgen Moltmann, in *God in Creation: A New Theology of Creation and the Spirit of God* (San Francisco: Harper & Row, 1985), 96, explains how the spirit that saves is also the spirit that sustains creation "and preserves it against annihilating Nothingness: 'When thou takest away their breath, they die and return to their dust. When thou sendest forth thy breath, they are created; and thou renewest the face of the ground' (Ps. 104:29–30). This means that the Spirit is the efficacious power of the Creator and the power that quickens created beings. . . . Through the presence of his own being, God preserves his creation against the annihilating Nothingness."

9. Wolfhart Pannenberg, *Systematic Theology* (Grand Rapids: Eerdmans, 1991), 2:76–77; see also 1:373.

is wildly exciting, if somewhat awkward. Yet even before that first kiss of life, we are alerted to the underside of creation: *adam*, like the animals, is dust from the ground. The new life, full and rich and pulsing with potential, is blown into someone who in short measure will be condemned to return to the earth, ashes to ashes, dust to dust (Gen. 3:19).

Like the rivers that extend from Eden to cover the earth's surface, the aching presence of death spreads through Israel's Scriptures. "As long as I live. . . . While I yet live" (Ps. 104:33). Death rides, in these simple phrases, along the edge of life. Israel's poets, the psalmists, grapple in particular with the realization that the spirit-breath is like a dike that holds death at bay. Princes and animals alike receive the life-giving spirit from God and give up their life, forfeit their plans (Ps. 146:4), and leave God's presence when that spirit—the *holy* spirit in Psalm 51—is taken away.

The drama and detail in Israel's sayings, stories, and poems should offer ample warning for us not to flatten stories and stanzas, not to reduce spirit to mere breath. Breath is the gift that God gives and takes away. Job demands that his friends ask the animals, the birds, the plants, and the fish, all of which know the basic truth that "the life of every living thing and the *rûaḥ* of every human being" is in God's hand (Job 12:10). Only the arrogant, such as Job's young and hostile companion Elihu, fail to reckon with their mortality and allow their arrogance to be transformed into a triumphalistic claim to superior knowledge. Elihu's reflections on mortality actually sound pious and uncannily like Job's: "The spirit of God has made me, and the breath of the Almighty gives me life. . . . See, before God I am as you are; I too was formed from a piece of clay" (Job 33:4, 6). While Elihu essentially finds common ground with Job, a deep divide separates Job's and Elihu's experiences of the spirit. Elihu's perspective is forged on the anvil of youth and health, untainted by age and debilitation, unscarred by sickness. Elihu, tired of listening to Job and his three older companions, is in the bloom of youth.

The true compass guiding Elihu's grasp of the spirit is his own inflated self-image. Elihu acknowledges the spirit within himself and sets *his* experience as the benchmark for all experiences: "The *rûaḥ* of God has made me," he claims, "and the breath of the Almighty gives me life" (Job 33:4). Elihu's perception of the spirit is shriveled and self-absorbed: the spirit of God has made *me*; the Almighty's breath gives *me* life. Elihu may be willing to admit with Job to a share in clay, but his sense of the spirit rises and falls on the breath given to *him*: the spirit creates *him*, and the breath gives *him* life.

Although Elihu sounds like Job—both realize that the spirit-breath is bordered by death—his words are a caricature, tinged as they are with a tenor of triumph. Elihu fails to acknowledge that he too will die when God takes back the spirit. Everyone else will die, including the rich and powerful and the likes of Job, but not Elihu. Perhaps Elihu should not be faulted for his ignorance. In the bulldozing verve of youth, Elihu has the spirit-breath in ample supply. He hasn't yet experienced the power of the spirit-breath to sustain life in the shadow of death. For all his claims to wisdom, therefore, Elihu's insight is paltry while Job's vision of the spirit in his deflated state is keen. Job has made his peace with the truth that the spirit-breath inspires him until it is eclipsed by death. Elihu has not.

The firmest fist raised in the face of death is by Israel's most flamboyant visionary, yet it is a fist that grows firmer with the passing of time, tighter with the looming presence of Babylon. Ezekiel's conviction crescendos with the increasingly catastrophic condition of Israel. While in his earlier years he appears at first to believe that individual Israelites can transform themselves, making for themselves a new heart and a new spirit, he abandons this hope in the wake of the disaster in Jerusalem in 587 BCE and finds himself not just in the valley of the shadow of death but in the valley of death itself, of very many dried and bleached bones heaped together. It is here where hope rises against hopelessness and where the visionary envisages the regathering and reforming of bones, sinews, and flesh followed by the infusion of the spirit-wind-breath—all three are one and the same *rûaḥ*—into them to bring new life to Israel. This is the new spirit and new heart that God promised. This is the new creation, the rescuing of life from death, the raising of the dead from their graves in order to cultivate the promised land once again. A new national body. A new spirit. A new Eden. A new creation altogether. And all of this in a valley of very many, very dry bones. The spirit accomplishes its most lavish task of re-creation, it would seem, in a grotesque valley of death.

Beyond Wisdom

Perhaps better than anyone else, the misguided figure Elihu inadvertently gets matters right—though he gets something else dead wrong when he suggests that the spirit functions best through spontaneity rather than study.

> And am I to wait, because they do not speak,
>> because they stand there, and answer no more?
> I also will give my answer;
>> I also will declare my opinion.
> For I am full of words;
>> the spirit [*rûaḥ*] within me constrains me.
> My heart is indeed like wine that has no vent;
>> like new wineskins, it is ready to burst.
> I must speak, so that I may find relief;
>> I must open my lips and answer. (Job 32:16–20)

Elihu is about to burst with spirit-breath. He has to say *something*. Unfortunately, his assumption is mistaken; he thinks the need to speak is the product of God's spirit-breath within rather than his own rash restlessness. He thinks that an excess of energy, a burst of words, equals a surplus of the spirit and sufficient wisdom. Elihu fails to recognize that the spirit-breath of the Almighty does not *automatically* make for understanding, that the *rûaḥ* in a mortal does not *inevitably* yield wisdom. Therefore, though he lays claim to inspiration, a sophomoric Elihu chides rather than encourages a disconsolate Job on the ash heap. What he says does not arise from discipline, from learning, from study; what he says arises from his own impatience and impetuosity.

The notion of the spirit in Israelite literature is far more closely aligned with the cultivation of skill and knowledge than Elihu cares to recognize. It demands a painstaking mastery of crafts and a stubborn pursuit of understanding. Joseph, for example, acquires knowledge through practice and experience in the home of Potiphar and in an Egyptian prison, where his leadership is so exceptional that everything is left in his hands. This experience comes to fruition in Joseph's ability to interpret Pharaoh's dream and to offer wholesale advice on how to hedge against the famine ahead. Pharaoh does not respond principally by commending Joseph's finely tuned skills; Pharaoh identifies in this man an incomparable spirit and consummate wisdom.[10]

This take on the spirit rises to the surface of eighth-century BCE prophecy in Micah's claim to be filled with the spirit—but not just the spirit: "I am filled with power, with the spirit of the LORD, and with justice and might." Micah knows that power and authority arise from clear-cut convictions cultivated over a lifetime (Mic. 3:1–8). In short, *Micah knows justice*, and not by dint of revelation. Because justice is learned, he can confront the people around him with the challenge that God "has told you, O mortal, what is good; and what does the LORD require of you but to do justice, and to love kindness, and to walk humbly with your God?" (Mic. 6:8). Justice is not revealed in dreams or visions; justice is read in Torah. Period.

Israel also remembered a symphony of skilled laborers, the wise of heart, who proved instrumental in the construction of the desert tent (Exod. 28:3). Bezalel and Oholiab, leaders in this skilled labor, are introduced as being filled not only with the spirit of God but with ability, intelligence, and knowledge in every kind of craft (Exod. 31:1–5; 35:31–35). They are reintroduced later as "filled with the spirit of wisdom" and "filled with wisdom of heart"—with wisdom and understanding of every craft (Exod. 36:1–3, my translation).[11] They are, in other words, chosen because they are highly skilled artisans in Israel. In the desert, God fills them to the brim with the spirit, not to learn new skills but to teach the skills they have already mastered through a lifetime of learning. Filling with the spirit represents the gathering up of a lifetime of learning and, with unprecedented intensity, pressing that skill into the service of a specific task. They are transported *through* wisdom *beyond* wisdom.

The association of wisdom and spirit explodes in the stories surrounding Daniel, an alien in foreign courts with an uncompromising commitment to Torah, to a simple life, and to education. The result of Daniel's discipline is stunning: a succession of influential foreign rulers recognize spirit and wisdom—both—to the nth degree within

10. The entire story of Joseph is found in Gen. 37; 39–45.
11. See also Exod. 31:1–5; 35:30–36:7.

him (Dan. 4:8–9 [MT 4:5–6]; 5:11–14; 6:3 [MT 6:4]). Once again, there is intensity here, a concentration of wisdom, a supersaturation of spirit. The spirit, in essence, brings Daniel's discipline to fruition.

This conception of *rûaḥ* as lifelong spirit-breath promises a robust understanding of charisma; the gift of the spirit from this perspective becomes less an endowment from the outside than an outburst of skills long learned and practiced. This understanding of *rûaḥ* in the Jewish Scriptures mirrors a point Pannenberg makes from a Christian perspective: "In an extended sense the breath of life that is already given to all of us at creation (Gen. 2:7) may be seen as endowment with God's Spirit. Beyond that, special manifestations in the course of life display specific and more intensive forms of endowment by God's Spirit, as in special capacities for insight, artistic gifts, prophetic inspiration, and leadership charisma."[12] This is a critical point: *the endowment of spirit-breath occasionally intensifies insight, artistic skill, prophecy, and leadership.*

Even when the spirit comes upon someone—that is, when it is not necessarily God's lifelong spirit-breath—the association of wisdom and spirit remains intact. Late in the eighth century BCE, the prophet Isaiah imagined an inspired and intelligent ruler upon whom the spirit would come to rest: "The spirit of the LORD shall rest on him, the spirit of wisdom and understanding, the spirit of counsel and might, the spirit of knowledge and the fear of the LORD" (Isa. 11:2). Punctuating this vision of wisdom, understanding, counsel, strength, knowledge, and fear of God is the word *rûaḥ*. Together these are the essential ingredients of robust rule. In Isaiah's imagination, there is no distinction between intelligence and inspiration. The resting presence of the spirit is the source of wisdom, knowledge, and understanding; Isaiah does not give the slightest indication that this resting of the spirit somehow ousts the ruler's intellect in blatant disregard for skills long refined.

It is difficult, given the preponderance of words, such as *understanding*, *wisdom*, *counsel*, and *knowledge*, coupled with a keen commitment to justice, to miss the point that the work of the spirit

12. Pannenberg, *Systematic Theology*, 3:9.

is tied in Isaiah 11 to learning. These are not charismatic endowments in the sense of gifts that come without preparation. It would be better to say that the ruler comes to the spirit with a predisposition for justice. In the end, it is not either-or. It is not a charismatic gift *or* human preparation that yields an effective reign. Where the spirit's work ends and human endeavor begins, where human learning ends and inspiration begins, cannot be pinpointed.

Finally, we encounter Amasai (1 Chron. 12:18), Azariah (2 Chron. 15:1), Jahaziel (20:14), and Zechariah (24:20–22) in an unexpected corner of the Jewish Scriptures: the books of 1–2 Chronicles, whose name, let alone the dull roar of countless genealogies at the start, is a deterrent to discovering inspiration in its pages. Still, these fabled four all receive the spirit and speak to those in power. The formula used to describe their inspiration comes straight from the book of Judges, where the spirit inspires heroic feats of liberation, but these latter-day speakers do not muster the troops and prepare for battle. In 1–2 Chronicles, inspired speakers deliver speeches that are rich in tradition, rife with citations and allusions, and, in the case of Jahaziel, set in the context of a priestly mandate. While the author is loath to indicate what exactly happens to these speakers when the spirit clothes or comes upon them—there are no details such as accompany Saul's experience of the spirit—there are enough clues to suggest that the primary purpose of inspiration by the spirit is to bring Israel's learned traditions to bear upon a contemporary situation. In Chronicles, the full scope of Scripture is incorporated in speeches that are at one and the same time inspired and instructive, spirit-directed and full of a nuanced interpretation of Scripture tailored to the demands of a concrete challenge.

Beyond Sacred Walls

Another realization brought to bear by a serious study of the Jewish Scriptures is so obvious by now that it should not need to be said: in the Bible, people other than Christians receive the spirit. The spirit is breathed into, comes upon, rests upon, pours out upon, fills, stands among, and leads people who are not Christians. Centuries before the birth of the church, Israelites laid conspicuous claim to the spirit—even the *holy* spirit.

Key figures in Israel possessed the spirit. Because they possessed this spirit, they were wise, capable, full of knowledge, and skilled. Joseph's ability to interpret dreams and, on a more practical level, to create a strategy for tackling a famine led Pharaoh to see in him a spirit of God. Bezalel could be so filled with the spirit of God, with knowledge and understanding, that he could teach the artisans exactly what they needed to know to build a spectacular tent for God's presence in the middle of the wilderness. Daniel could have within him *spirit* to the nth degree for so long that three generations of foreign rulers could attribute *wisdom* to the nth degree to him.

The judges and Israel's first king, Saul, received the spirit and liberated their people (Judg. 3:10; 6:34; 11:29; 14:6, 19; 15:14; 1 Sam. 11:6). Protégés Joshua and Elisha received the spirit from their mentors (Num. 27:18; Deut. 34:9; 2 Kings 2:9, 15–16). Prophets—Micah, Isaiah, Ezekiel, and a prophet of the exile (Isa. 40–55)—claimed the spirit in various guises and spoke so perspicuously that, despite resistance during their own day, their words were embraced by later editors. One of these prophets even promised a gifted ruler, upon whom the spirit would rest (Isa. 11:1–9).

The whole nation of Israel received another promise: the spirit outpoured (Isa. 32:15; 44:3; Ezek. 39:28–29). The transformation would be wild, the metamorphosis dumbfounding. The nation as a whole would be refreshed, though Zechariah constricts the outpouring to an elite segment of Israelite society, not to privilege them but to impel them to grief and ultimately reconciliation (Zech. 12:10). Another prophet, Joel, imagined an outpouring over all flesh—throughout a world beyond Israel's borders, where slave girls would prophesy, where young and old alike would see visions and dream dreams (Joel 2:28–32; MT 3:1–5). This is not a world bound by church or doctrine, creed or community. The spirit outpoured tears down walls.

This smattering of texts uncovers a misguided assumption deftly identified by Christian Pentecostal theologian Frank Macchia, in which "the Spirit in the Old Testament is thus usually viewed as a fleeting and inadequate foretaste of the supernatural Spirit given through Christ, punctuated by momentary and noteworthy endowments, but generally experienced within a situation of relative spiritual dearth while awaiting the fullness of the Spirit that came through Christ. The possibility that we have overlooked in the Old Testament a rich understanding of spiritual fullness that is not well represented in the New Testament should give us pause to think."[13]

In order to sustain this view of the spirit as a Christian reality against the evidence of the Jewish Scriptures, it is necessary for some Christians to introduce distinctions between the testaments. The spirit in the Jewish Scriptures, for instance, is thought to be only an *intermittent* presence and the spirit in the New Testament a *permanent* one. This point of view cannot stand in light of countless texts in the Jewish Scriptures: the artisans whose lifelong cultivation of the spirit of wisdom bursts on the scene in the desert (Exod. 28:3), David's possession of the spirit (1 Sam. 16:13), Isaiah's imagined inspired ruler upon whom the spirit rests (Isa. 11:1–9), and Haggai's conviction that the spirit stands in Israel's midst (Hag. 2:5), to name a few.

The equally convenient but misleading distinction between the spirit as a *power* in the Old Testament and a *person* in the New evaporates in the face of the lament in Isaiah 63:7–14, in which the spirit takes on the role of the angel of God's presence in order to lead Israel to the promised land. In a similar way, Haggai's promise portrays the spirit standing in Israel's midst, like the pillars that led and protected Israel in its earliest days (Hag. 2:5). It may be possible to employ such distinctions between a power and a person in an ill-conceived effort to preserve an exclusive Christian claim to the spirit, but such an effort would demand a conscious neglect of pivotal Old Testament texts.

For this reason, Macchia makes an impassioned plea to his Pentecostal community that is relevant to all Christians. "As revivalists," he writes,

> we bathe in the glow of born again Christianity and accent even more than other Evangelicals the supernatural character of the Spirit's presence as a gift given to those who embrace Christ by faith. This accent

13. Frank Macchia, "The Spirit of Life and the Spirit of Immortality: An Appreciative Review of Levison's *Filled with the Spirit*," *Pneuma* 33 (2011): 72.

on the supernatural and eschatological nature of the filling of the Spirit is not problematic in itself, except we tend to think that we can only highlight this by neglecting the Spirit that inspires human wisdom and virtue "from below," so to speak. We thus tend to see life outside of (or prior to) Christ as dark, lost, and devoid of the Holy Spirit.[14]

There was darkness in Israel. Lostness too. But Israel held tenaciously to a belief in the spirit's ability to be inbreathed, to come upon, to rest upon, to be passed on, to be poured out, to fill, to stand, and to guide. No single impression of the spirit dominated the skyline, but the seamless conviction that God was present through the spirit threaded through Israel's experience of darkness. In fact, this conviction grew especially in times of crisis, when darkness threatened to overwhelm Israel. Isaiah, resisted by ignorant and ambitious kings who failed to grasp the fallibility of the political alliances they pursued, promised an inspired ruler. Ezekiel, bereft in Babylon, amassed more glimmers of the spirit than any other single writer. Haggai, in the desperation of return from exile, promised the spirit's standing in Israel's midst. The book of Daniel, generated by the terrors of Greek overlords, devotes three chapters to a man both disciplined and inspired, both spirited and wise. Yes, Israel knew darkness, but that darkness did not eclipse belief in the spirit's ability to liberate, to invigorate, and to decontaminate a polluted nation. That darkness, in fact, seems to have spawned an enduring conviction that the spirit, if not now, then one day, would be present in Israel yet again.

Beyond Spirituality

This *rûaḥ*, we have seen, devastates misleading dichotomies. The distinction between breath and spirit will not stand. Nor will the bifurcation of male and female. Nor can creation versus salvation— *spiritus vivificans* and *spiritus sanctificans*. The contrast between learning and inspiration, too, crumbles in the face of *rûaḥ*. Perhaps the most salient dichotomy this *rûaḥ* defies is the one between religion and politics. The spirit, in short, is not *spiritual* in any sort of

14. Macchia, "Spirit of Life," 71.

parochial or individualistic or solipsistic way. A casual glance over Israel's Scriptures puts the lie to any attempt to sequester the spirit within a private sphere. The spirit is ubiquitous in public life, in politics, in society. Verb after verb gives broad testimony to the *public* presence of the spirit.

Coming upon. When the spirit comes upon figures in the Jewish Scriptures, what transpires is invariably public. Balaam resists the pressure of King Balak and offers a blessing upon the fledgling nation of Israel, which is poised to take the promised land (Num. 24:2). Biblical judges gather troops or, like Gideon, winnow them, and bring victory over Israel's oppressors (Judg. 3:10; 6:34; 11:29; 14:6, 19; 15:14). Saul, too, fills his role as military leader when the spirit comes upon him (1 Sam. 11:6). Even while the four figures of 1–2 Chronicles eschew military solutions and strategies, they offer public words intended to safeguard the survival of Israel (1 Chron. 12:18; 2 Chron. 15:1; 20:14; 24:20–22).[15] When the spirit comes upon an individual, then, what occurs is public, whether by way of benediction or battle. The spirit does not kindle a private devotion.

Resting upon. When the spirit rests upon the seventy-two elders in the desert, it is to help Moses administrate the unwieldy refugees from Egypt. He needs help; through the shared experience of a vision reminiscent of their prior experience at Mount Sinai, Israel's elders reestablish the authority of Moses, if only temporarily (Num. 11:16–30). In a powerful prophetic text, Isaiah's imagined inspired root of Jesse, upon whom the spirit rests, is keen to impose an equitable reign that extends even to the animal world, so that wolves lie down with lambs, leopards with goats, calves with lions, cows with bears, and babies with snakes (Isa. 11:6–9). A transformation of the cosmos, a toppling of the world order, is generated by a Davidic king: "with righteousness he shall judge the poor, and decide with equity for the meek of the earth; he shall strike the earth with the rod of his mouth, and with the *rûaḥ* of his lips he shall kill the wicked. Righteousness shall be the belt around his waist, and faithfulness the belt around his loins" (11:4–5). This is hardly a private vision of a soul transformed by the regenerative work of the holy spirit; it is cosmic

---

15. 2 Chron. 24:20–22 may be the sole exception to this pattern.

in scope, the work of a king on whom the spirit of the Lord rests, "the spirit of wisdom and understanding, the spirit of counsel and might, the spirit of knowledge and the fear of the LORD" (11:2). The focus of the inspired servant is no less public; the servant will bring justice not just to Israel but to the coastland: "He will not grow faint or be crushed until he has established justice in the earth; and the coastlands wait for his teaching" (42:1–9, quoting v. 4). Along the same vein, a prophet later in the book of Isaiah claims the anointing of the spirit in order "to bring good news to the oppressed, to bind up the brokenhearted, to proclaim liberty to the captives, and release to the prisoners; to proclaim the year of the LORD's favor, and the day of vengeance of our God." Those who mourn in Zion will build—rebuild—Zion's ruins. This too is a public event, lush with garlands and oil and oaks of justice (61:1–4, quoting vv. 1–2). When the spirit comes to rest, the impact cannot be wrestled into privacy. Whole arenas of existence, extending from Israel's poor to far-flung nations to the hostile world of animals, will come to a unique harmony when the spirit rests on equally unique leaders, political and prophetic—both.

Passing on. Not even the passing of the spirit from one person to another is an entirely private affair. When Moses lays his hands upon Joshua, he transfers the spirit so that Joshua can lead Israel (Deut. 34:9), which he does with a vengeance as he splits the promised land into thirds and conquers it. When Zedekiah slaps and derides Micaiah ben Imlah, wondering how the spirit passed from one to the other, the issue is a word spoken to the king—a word, in fact, spoken about the king's imminent public death in an ill-conceived battle. The spirit passed from Zedekiah to Micaiah to condemn the strategy of going to war (1 Kings 22:24–25).[16] When Elisha receives a double portion of Elijah's spirit, the protégé does even more remarkable miracles in Israel than his mentor (2 Kings 2:9–14). The spirit, in short, inspires Elisha to be Israel's prophet, a keenly public figure who ably resists king and queen, as did Elijah.

16. Micaiah responds to Zedekiah with rich irony: "You will find out on that day when you go in to hide in an inner chamber." Micaiah's public statement about the king's death contrasts with what Zedekiah will do when he is forced to retreat in a hideout because he is wrong about the impending battle.

Outpouring. The national and global impact of the spirit is just as apparent in the passages that predict an outpouring of the spirit. In the earliest oracle, Isaiah predicts desolation and grief "until a spirit from on high is poured out on us, and the wilderness becomes a fruitful field, and the fruitful field is deemed a forest." Then, and only then, "justice will dwell in the wilderness, and righteousness abide in the fruitful field. The effect of righteousness will be peace, and the result of righteousness, quietness and trust forever" (Isa. 32:15–17). Expectations from the period of exile offer their own particular twist on this theme. A prophet in the line of Isaiah offers what looks like a traditional hope—"I will pour my spirit upon your descendants, and my blessing on your offspring"—but with the possibility that others, *foreigners*, will also adopt the name of Israel (Isa. 44:3–5, quoting v. 3). For Ezekiel, the hope is national in scope: God will pour out the spirit on the house of Israel, gather Israel to its own land, and—in a promise that shatters divine reticence—not hide God's presence-face anymore. Revelation is massive, exposure to the divine immense, even if it is limited to Israel (Ezek. 39:28–29). The prophet Joel takes this vision in the opposite direction: to all flesh. Unbounded, the spirit inspires prophecy, dreams, and visions, not to a slender elite at the top of society, as in the story of Moses and the elders in the desert (Num. 11), but to old and young alike in an outpouring that will reach even to "male and female slaves." The day will be cataclysmic in the heavens, too, with epiphanies reminiscent of the smoke and fire on Mount Sinai, though now "everyone who calls on the name of the Lord shall be saved" (Joel 2:28–32; MT 3:1–5). Finally, most narrowly but arguably most dramatically, a spirit of favor or compassion will be poured over only the house of David and the inhabitants of Jerusalem in the small Persian province of Yehud. Yet what an impact this outpouring will have! Political leaders who instigated a violent crime will mourn and weep for the one they pierced with the intensity of someone who has lost an only child (Zech. 12:10). The spirit, in short, will bring about public, *political* reconciliation. Each of these predictions of the spirit outpoured has its own distinctive hue, yet all of them without exception share a conviction that the spirit outpoured has an immense impact upon the public sphere, where politics and spirituality collide—or, more peaceably construed, coincide.

Filling. When the spirit fills individuals, the impact is invariably public. Joseph and Daniel, representing some of the earliest and latest stories in the Jewish Scriptures, are mirror images of each other (Gen. 41:38; Dan. 4:8–9 [MT 4:5–6]; 5:11–14; 6:3 [MT 6:4]). Both heroes survive impressively in hostile environments, and both distinguish themselves with an extraordinary wisdom that propels them to the upper echelons of foreign courts. Consequently, foreign rulers from Egypt, Babylon, and Media, rather than Israelite insiders, recognize the spirit within Joseph and Daniel. The spirit also fills artisans in the desert for a different sort of public action: building a tent. They are filled to the brim in order to build or, in the case of Bezalel and Oholiab, to teach others the skills to build (Exod. 28:3; 31:1–5; 35:30–36:7, esp. 35:34 on teaching). The product is physical, the result material: a tent in the desert, a palpable sign of God's presence, a tangible abode for God's glory. Add to these an autobiographical claim to the spirit within. The prophet Micah's call for justice is rooted in a prophetic call: "I am filled with power, with the spirit of the LORD, and with justice and might, to declare to Jacob his transgression and to Israel his sin" (Mic. 3:8). A public vocation inspired by the spirit lies at the heart of Micah's conviction. Like Micaiah ben Imlah, Micah puts his reputation on the line in his appeal to justice. Public, all of these. Even when the spirit is deep within individuals, the purpose is public: ruling in foreign courts, building a tent in the desert, proclaiming justice, and exposing Israel's sins.

Cleansing. Even this sort of activity is not a private affair. Ezekiel's promise of a new heart and spirit tangles with Israel's recalcitrance; the fate of the nation as a whole is at stake (Ezek. 11:17–21; 18:30–32; 36:22–28). These are not private matters. Even the individual lament in Psalm 51 was understood as the plea of a wayward king: David had taken Bathsheba and murdered her husband. Now the king begs for forgiveness, for purity, for integrity. This ascription is only traditional, but it reveals nonetheless how an intensely private poem could have intensely *public* consequences.

Standing and guiding. The public sphere is also palpable in the promise of Haggai and the lament of Isaiah 63. In fact, the whole point of Haggai's promise is that the spirit is public, standing like the pillar of the exodus among the people now called to rebuild Jerusalem

(Hag. 2:5). In the same way, the spirit's public presence is central to the lament in Isaiah 63, where the angel of God's presence, which led Israel from Egypt to the promised land, is swiftly identified as the holy spirit in Israel's midst—a spirit Israel had resisted even as they had resisted the angel that led them. Still, this spirit, like the presence of God, now gives Israel rest. Nothing could be more public: these are the tangible if invisible signs of God's presence (Isa. 63:7–14).

In light of the Jewish Scriptures, a spirituality that impels a retreat from public engagement is not an authentic spirituality at all. The spirit exercises a considerable impact over the nation, even over the entire world, from old to young, male to female, elite to impoverished. An experience of the spirit that does not bend the arc of this world toward justice, at least from the perspective of the Jewish Scriptures, is not a genuine experience at all. That sort of spirituality is an escape rather than the durable stuff of the spirit, whose presence changes the world upon which it rushes and rests, through which it passes, on which it is outpoured, which it fills, and in which it stands as guide and guardian.

The process of discerning the spirit in the public sphere may be disconcerting, disquieting, even distressing; it is safer to sequester the spirit within the sphere of private spirituality. Discerning the spirit in the public sphere is far more demanding a task: rulers bend in different directions, integrity is rarely worn on a politician's sleeve, the choice is often between two evils rather than good and evil. Yet that is the sphere in which the spirit exercises an inexorable impact. For all of its ambiguity, therefore, for all of the thorny ethical questions it may raise, this is the *rûah* that a reader of the Old Testament encounters.

Beyond Scarcity

Job's young friend Elihu understands that the spirit does not trickle down to the wise; the spirit exists in such measure, with such force, that it holds a sage hostage, laying siege-works against him. His heart is like a wineskin about to burst (Job 32:8–20).

Elihu's claims, misguided though they may be, uncover what may have been a presumption of Israelite belief in the spirit. Though we must tread lightly when we speak of this because of the paucity of data, we should not for that reason avoid the implication altogether that the spirit was understood as some sort of material presence. Elihu feels he must either speak or burst because the spirit-breath in him lays siege-works against him. Micah has a slew of words that roll over his tongue, while false prophets have no spirit-breath rolling over theirs because they have stopped their mouths with their hands (Mic. 3:7–8). The artisans and their teachers, Bezalel and Oholiab, are believed to possess an excess of this spirit-breath because they are so knowledgeable, so conspicuously competent, in all sorts of crafts (Exod. 28:3; 31:1–5; 35:30–36:7). Joshua too can receive the vitality that is in Moses—physical, tangible vitality—when Moses's hand(s) rests upon him (Deut. 34:9). Elisha, for his part, demands of his mentor, Elijah, a double portion of his spirit (2 Kings 2:9). Finally, Daniel's extraordinary wisdom is identified with a surfeit of spirit-breath in him (Dan. 4:8–9 [MT 4:5–6]; 5:11–14; 6:3 [MT 6:4]).

Whether or not the spirit was ultimately understood as a material presence that filled particularly gifted individuals, Elihu's sensation of compulsion goes a long way toward explaining why select Israelites are depicted as full or filled with the spirit. This is lavish language because these are not individuals who follow God half-heartedly.

Micah, for example, contrasts the mouths of his opponents with his own. These prophets, from Micah's perspective, live in a world of emptiness, a world without vision, without sun, without an answer from God, without a word on their lips. Micah's world, in contrast, is full of power, spirit of the Lord, justice, and might. The force of Micah's parataxis becomes especially lavish—power, spirit of the Lord, justice, and might—in comparison with the empty-mouthed prophets, over whose tongues no breath will flow and whose lips are covered by their hands.

Pharaoh's question in the presence of Joseph implies a lavish underbelly, a rich draft that rises from within Joseph: "Can we find anyone else like this—one in whom is the spirit of God?" (Gen. 41:38). The sages and magicians of Egypt are captive to their ignorance. Joseph alone solves the conundrum of Pharaoh's dream and then without external prompting takes the initiative to devise a successful strategy for survival that would serve the common good. Joseph alone, of all the leaders in Egypt, mirrors the divine world with a full measure of discernment and wisdom.

This lavishness of spirit continues in the midst of Israel's recalcitrance and the desert's desolation, where Israelites en masse offer much more than is needed until Moses is compelled to tell them to stop, where hearts are prompted and spirits lifted to offer with unmatched munificence even more than is necessary to build a tent for God in the wilderness (Exod. 36:1–7). There are others as well—artisans, the wise of heart—who are filled with the spirit of wisdom. The materials from which they spin and hammer are depicted with bright colors, vivid hues, and brilliant detail. This is all part of the lavish tapestry that contributes to the tent of presence—an extravagant scene that contrasts with the void of Sinai, the impatience of Israel, and the debacle of the golden calf (Exod. 32–40).

Only a language of surfeit can describe people whose skills are extraordinary and expansive in a narrative that is preoccupied with a singularly unrepeatable moment in Israel's history. Small wonder that their leaders Bezalel and Oholiab are described as being *filled* with (the) spirit of God and wisdom of heart, and with an additional cumbersome parataxis that drips with lavish praise: Bezalel was filled with the spirit of God, wisdom, intelligence, and knowledge. Here in the unyielding wilderness of Sinai, there is inexplicable excess, an imposing generosity, a stunning collection of skills, a fullness marked by adept artisans who exhibit extraordinary craftsmanship and, no less salient, hearts at the ready to teach (Exod. 28:3; 31:1–5; 35:30–36:7).

Even one bare-boned depiction of Joshua characterizes him in a way that is reminiscent of the grandeur of Joseph as "a man in whom is the spirit" (Num. 27:18). The other brief depiction suggests perhaps that Joshua first was filled with a spirit of wisdom when Moses laid his hands upon him (Deut. 34:9). Joshua took over from Moses, of whom it can be said that even at one hundred and twenty years of age "his sight was not dimmed and his vigor had not abated" (Deut. 34:7). In a touching scene when Moses lays his hands on Joshua, a young man receives from an aging mentor a surge of vigor, of vitality, of wisdom, of *rûaḥ*.

The stories of Daniel in foreign courts galvanize these strands. There may be no parataxis, as in Micah's claim to power and justice or the description of Bezalel, but three successive narratives about three successive reigns call attention to his extraordinary wisdom and knowledge. Throughout these stories, he garners enormous praise, for he, like Joseph, is both an unparalleled interpreter of the inscrutable and an administrator par excellence. And why? Because in him is God-given spirit to the nth degree—an extraordinary measure of the divine vitality that is the source of knowledge and wisdom.

Lavish and lush. Excess. Even glut. Pure glut. This is the world of the spirit. When the spirit appears, Obadiah knows, a prophet like Elijah may be plucked up and thrown onto another mountain altogether. This is a world oddly reconceived.

When the spirit rushes upon people, they do something significant, whether rallying the troops to confront oppressors (Judg. 3:10; 6:34; 11:29; 1 Sam. 11:6) or gathering the traditions in a strategic word spoken to those in power (1 Chron. 12:18; 2 Chron. 15:1; 20:14; 24:20–22). This is a world lavishly reconceived.

When the spirit rests, the axis of the world shifts as wolves and lambs lie together (Isa. 11:1–9), a light of teaching casts a shadow far past the coastlands (42:1–9), and the poor wear victory garlands (61:1–4). This is not a world with wild animals safe in cages, with shadowy caves half-lit, with prisoners fed leftovers. This is a world lavishly reconceived top to bottom.

When the spirit is outpoured, deserts become fields and fields forests (Isa. 32:15; 44:3), criminals moan in grief (Zech. 12:10), slave girls prophesy (Joel 2:28–32; MT 3:1–5). This is a world lavishly reconceived bottom to top.

When men and women receive new hearts and new spirits, they are not somewhat clean, lightly polished. They are splattered with water, scrubbed into purity. Their stony hearts are torn from their chests so that they can receive a heart of flesh, pulsing with devotion (Ezek. 36:22–28). This is a world lavishly reconceived inside out.

When Israel faces daunting challenges, when they are faint with fear, the spirit stands guard as in the days—the single night, rather—when the pillar stood on the shore of the sea, protecting the earliest of Israel's refugees from the onslaught of the Egyptian army (Hag. 2:5). Even when Israel yearns for that spirit, the memory is not distant, detached, or diminished. The memory is vivid of the holy spirit that proved unremitting in leading Israel to the promised land in the face of their rebellion (Isa. 63:7–14). This is a world lavishly reconceived start to finish.

This dimension of the spirit does not bring us any closer to the meaning—the semantic range—of the word *rûaḥ*. It does not clarify whether we should understand *rûaḥ* as breath, wind, spirit, or Spirit in any given instance. It does not elucidate the phenomena, ecstatic or not, that attended Israelite prophecy. It does not ultimately cinch the question of whether the Israelites conceived of the spirit as a patently material reality. Still, it does say something, however elusive, about the spirit, whose presence yields lavish results in times of scarcity, lavish hope in times of despair, lavish memories in times of misery. The spirit lingers like the spirit of Eliphaz's nightmare, on the edge of anguish, poised to come, to rest, to be passed along, to be outpoured, to fill, to stand, and to guide. That is why, when Ezekiel prophesies in that desperate valley of very many, very bleached bones, the spirit-winds come rushing, without hesitancy or hiatus, to rattle those bones nearly back to life. All that is left, all that is needed, is a single, final puff of spirit-breath. When that occurs, it is not just a few stragglers who come to life. The results are lavish, enough to rattle a valley of bones, transforming them into an entire army come to life.

Or perhaps that lavishness comes to us disguised on an ash heap, where a defeated man is the unwilling object of theological inquiry. There, scratching himself with the sharp edges of broken pots, sits Job, a torment to his wife, a plague to his friends. His breath is thin, his spirit shallow in his chest—yet not so thin or shallow as to prevent him from whispering, "as long as breath is in me and the *rûaḥ* of God is in my nostrils, my lips will not speak falsehood, and my tongue will not utter deceit" (Job 27:3–4). He may be mistaken, but he will not betray the truth. He may fail, but he will not forfeit his integrity. There is no obvious surfeit of the spirit here, but there is a determination, a tenacity, a penchant for the truth, integrity, and honesty. This is itself a small outpouring of the spirit, even if there is little left of that spirit in Job, who knows that inspiration survives, perhaps even thrives, in the shadows, below the cliffs of despair.

Scripture and Ancient Sources Index

Subject Index